CW00422050

Bruce McLean & William Alsop, Malagarba Works.

WILEY-ACADEMY

rock

①　②　③　④

⑤　⑥　⑦　⑧

Bruce & Lill working on
Berlin in MENORCA.

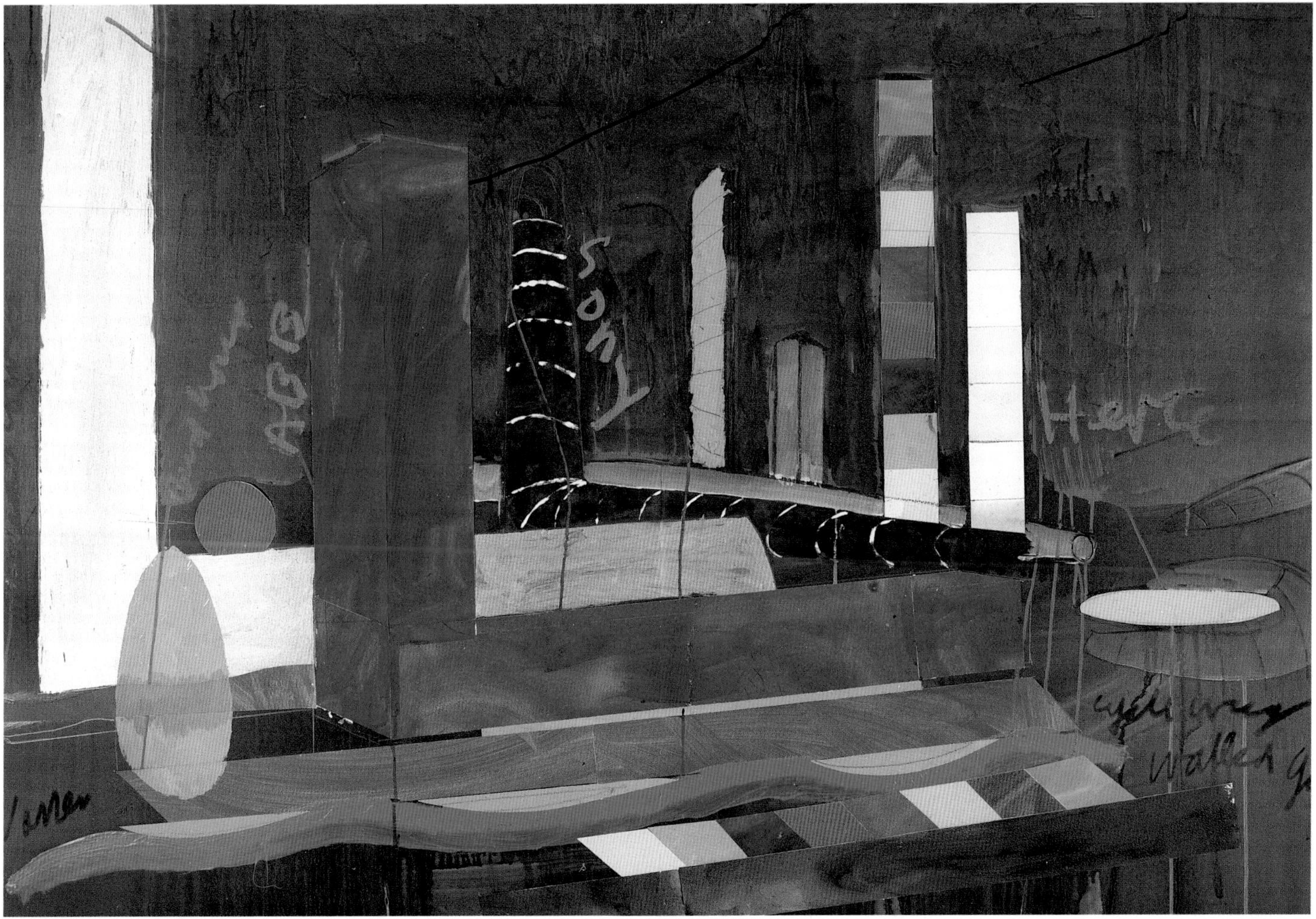
SONY
Here

a

city as

opera

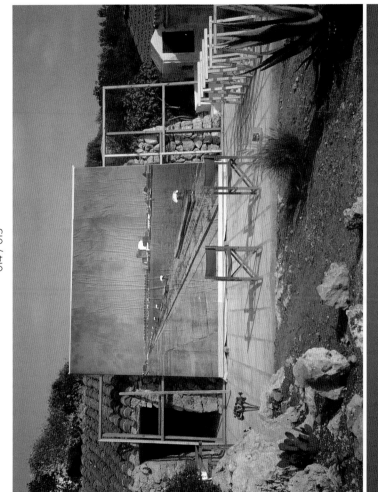

```
          silo
grain     silo
un-       used
sil       (opera)
          operations
                              at      all      times to all people

a         view    across the water
a         view    up from inside

a         set for all seasons       at      all      times of day

a         place   to                capture the imagination
a         place   to      rush      through
a         place   to      rush
                  to

          the proposition emerges from looking a large pictures and changing them
          it is the city of imagined possibility
          the city that has only to be enjoyed
          not understood
sil-      opera
```

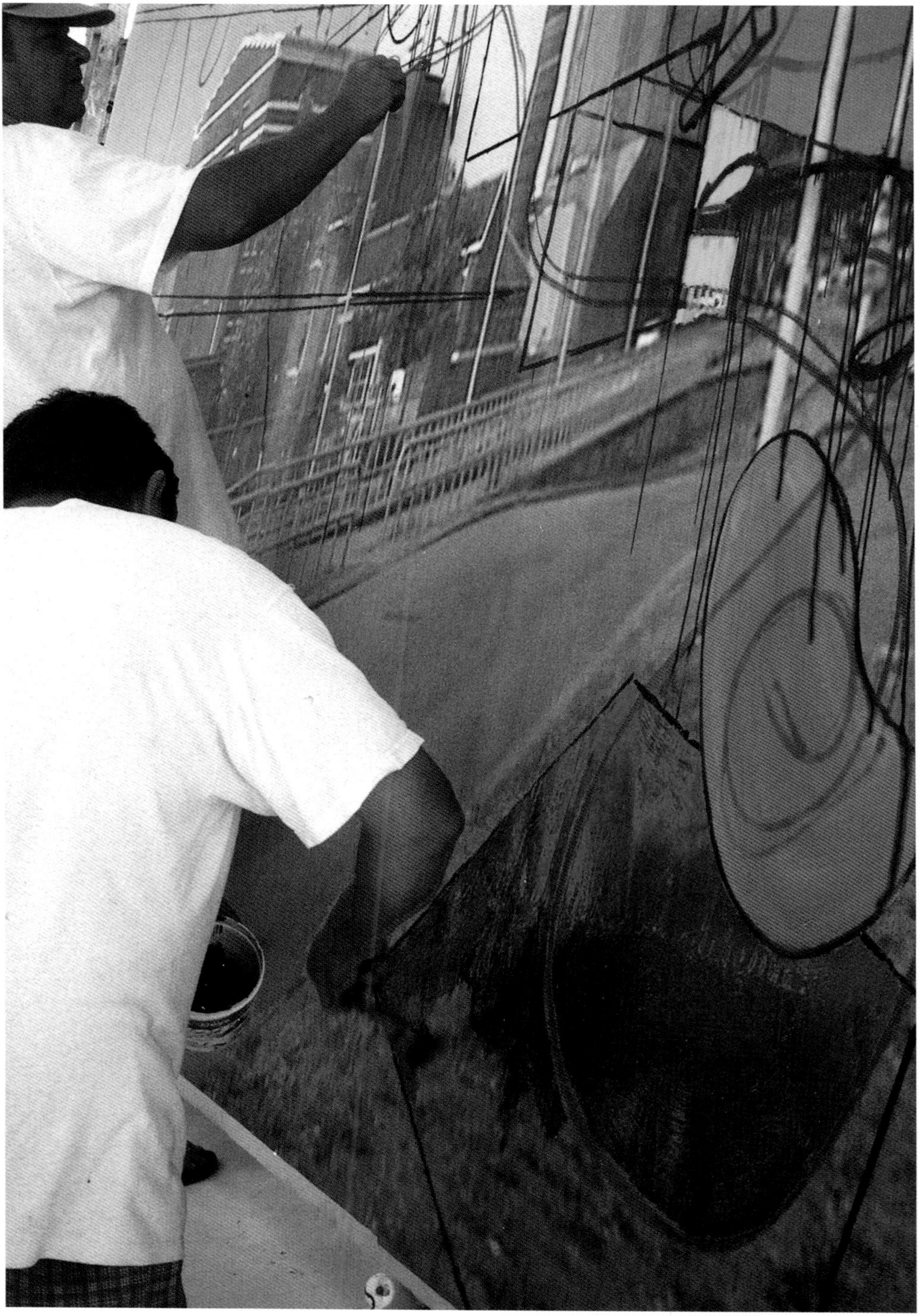

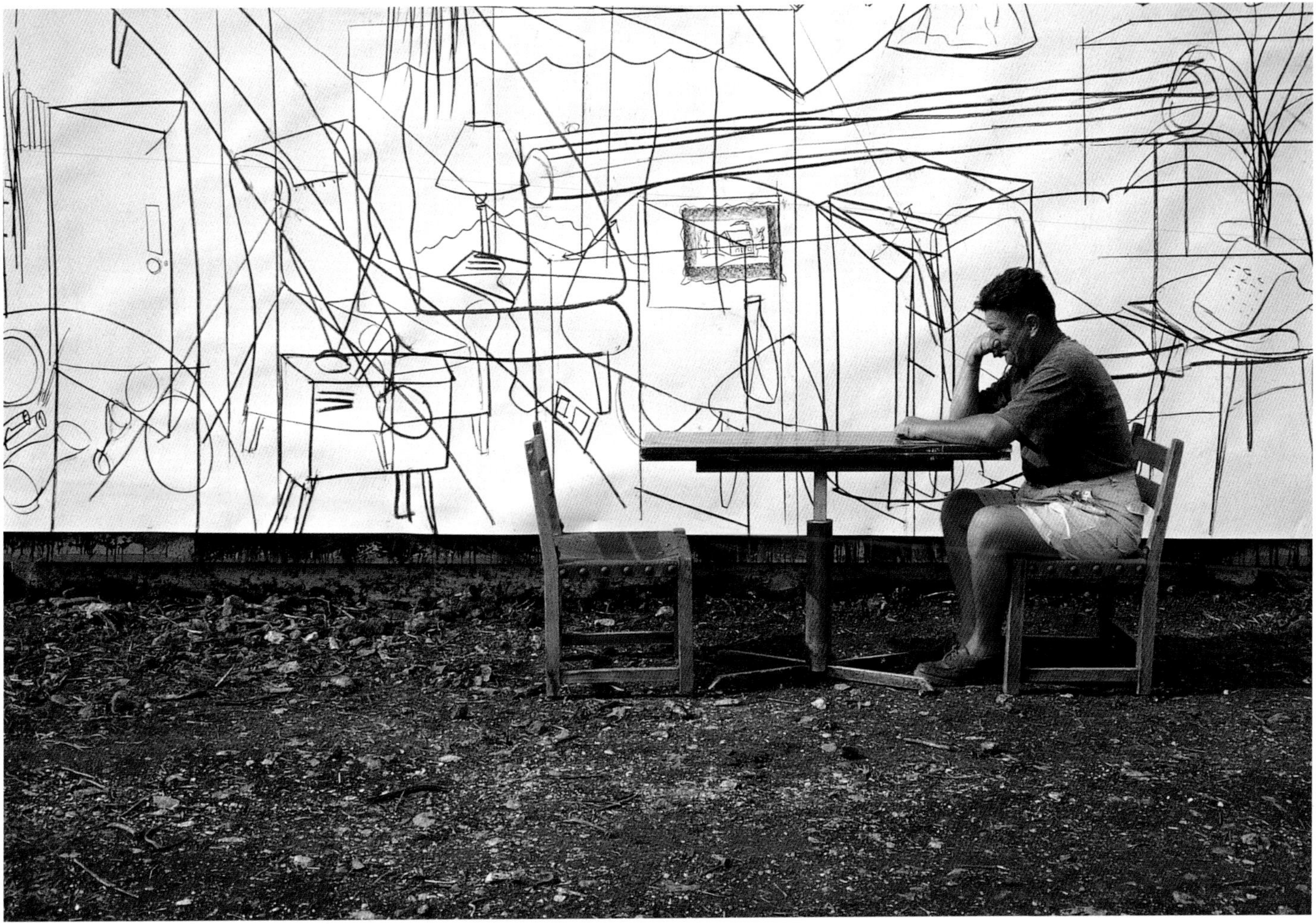

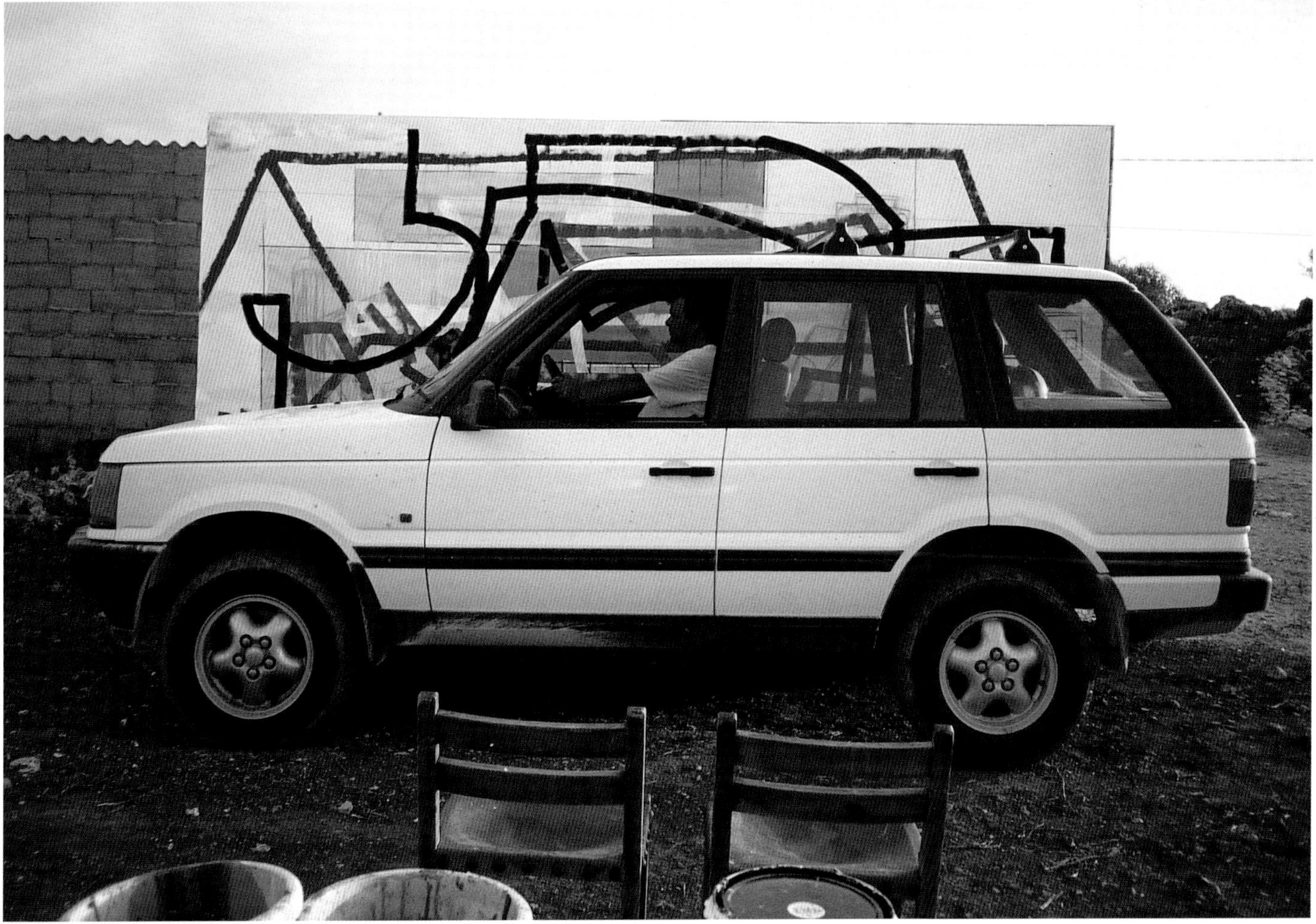

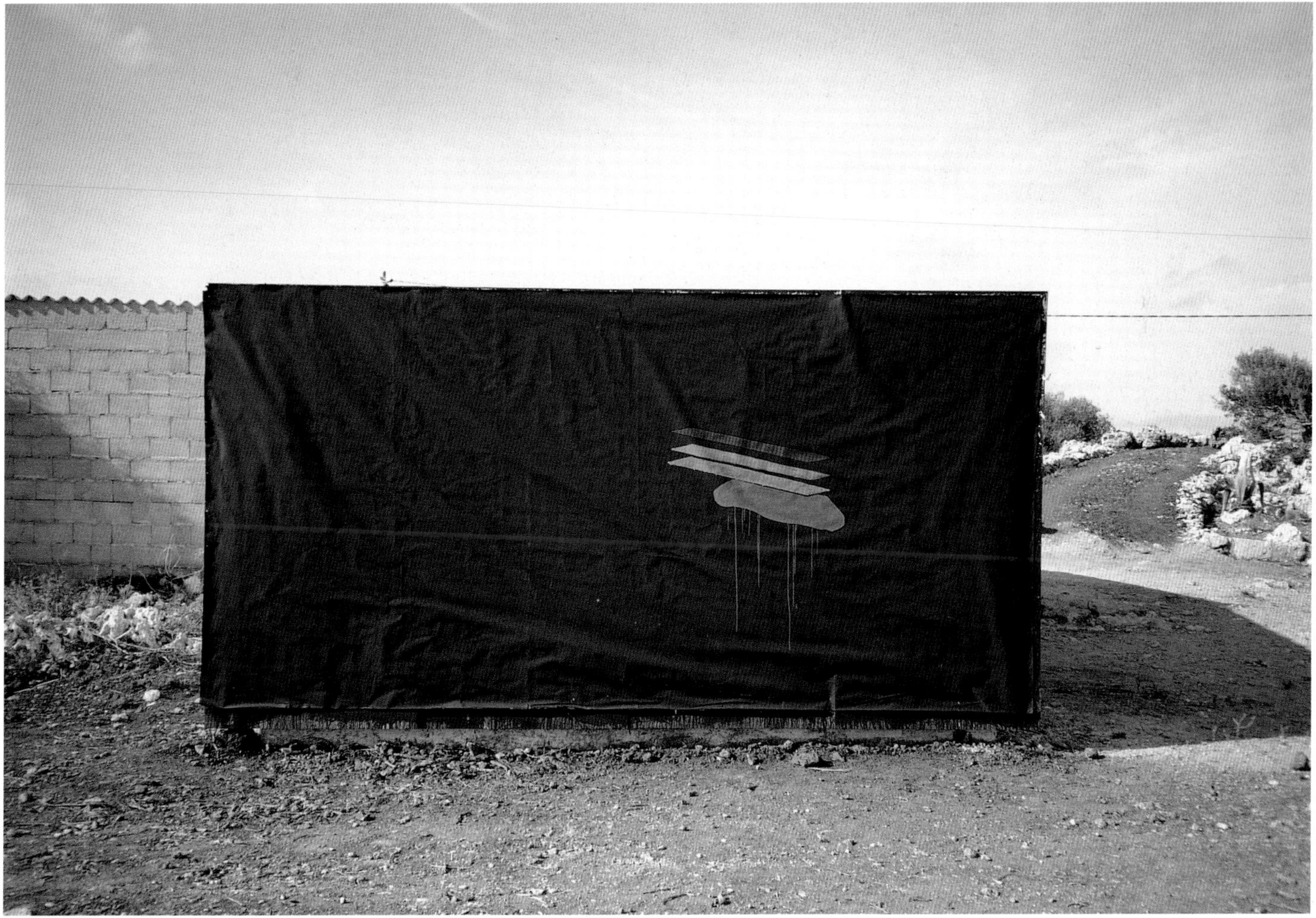

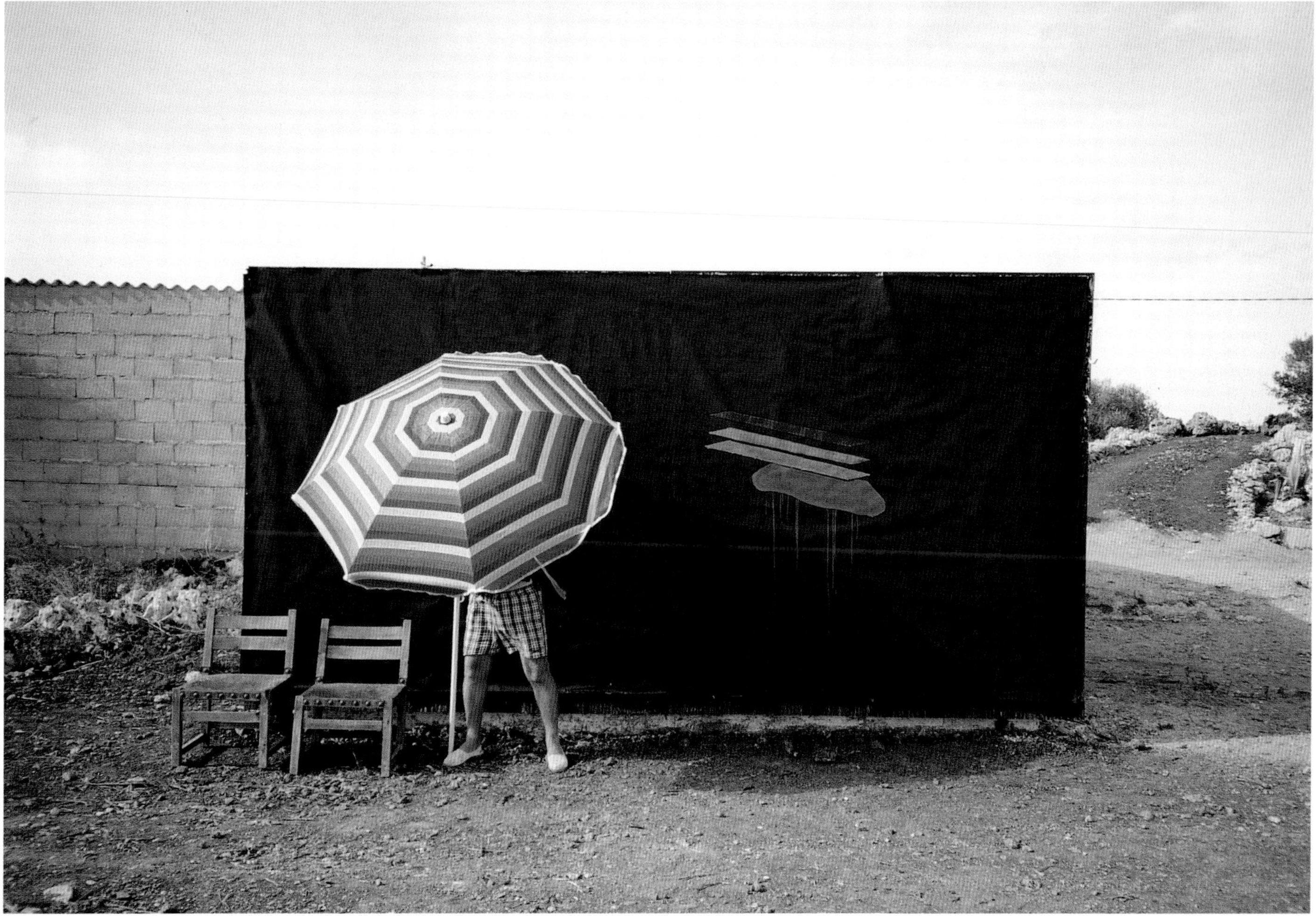

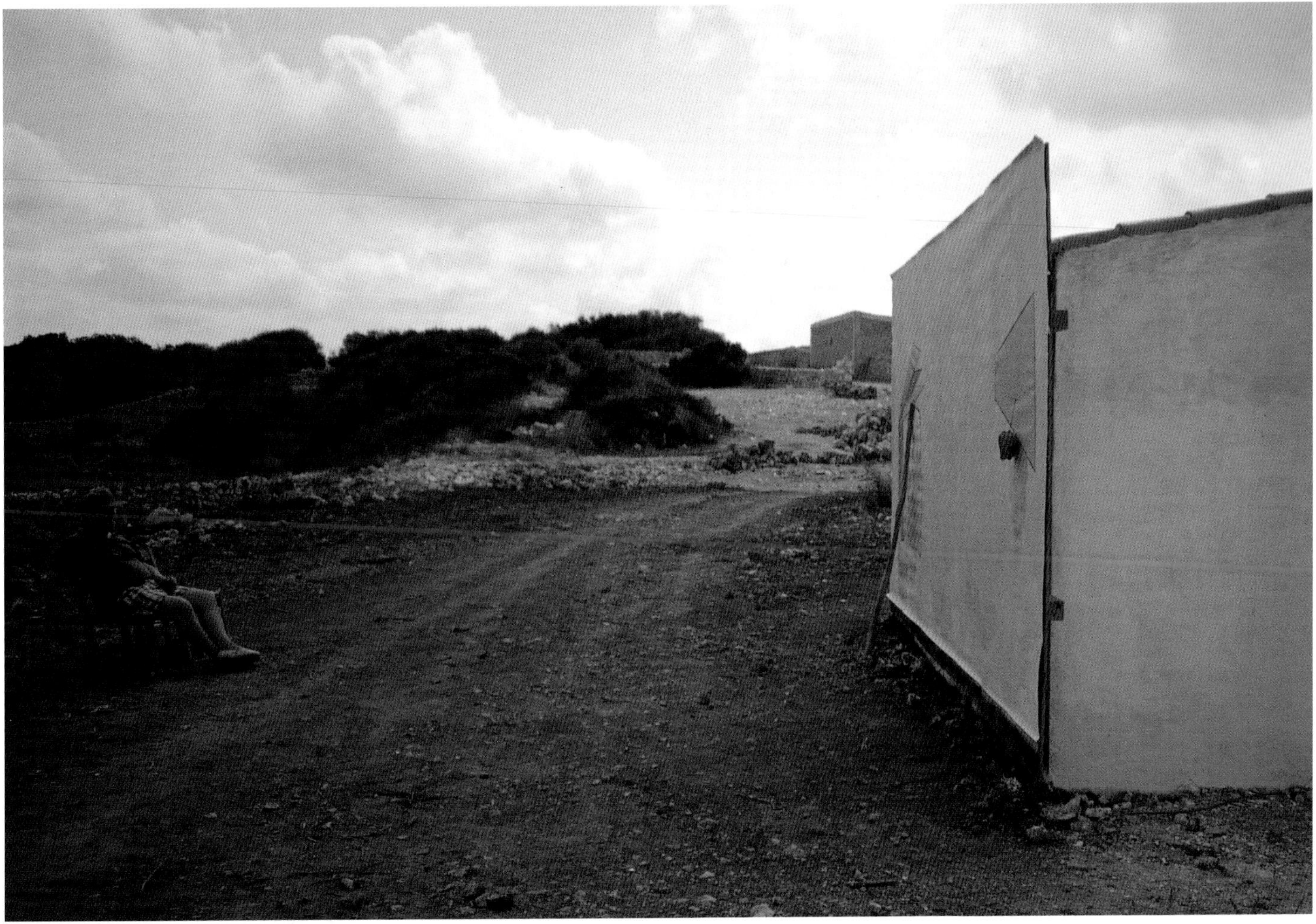

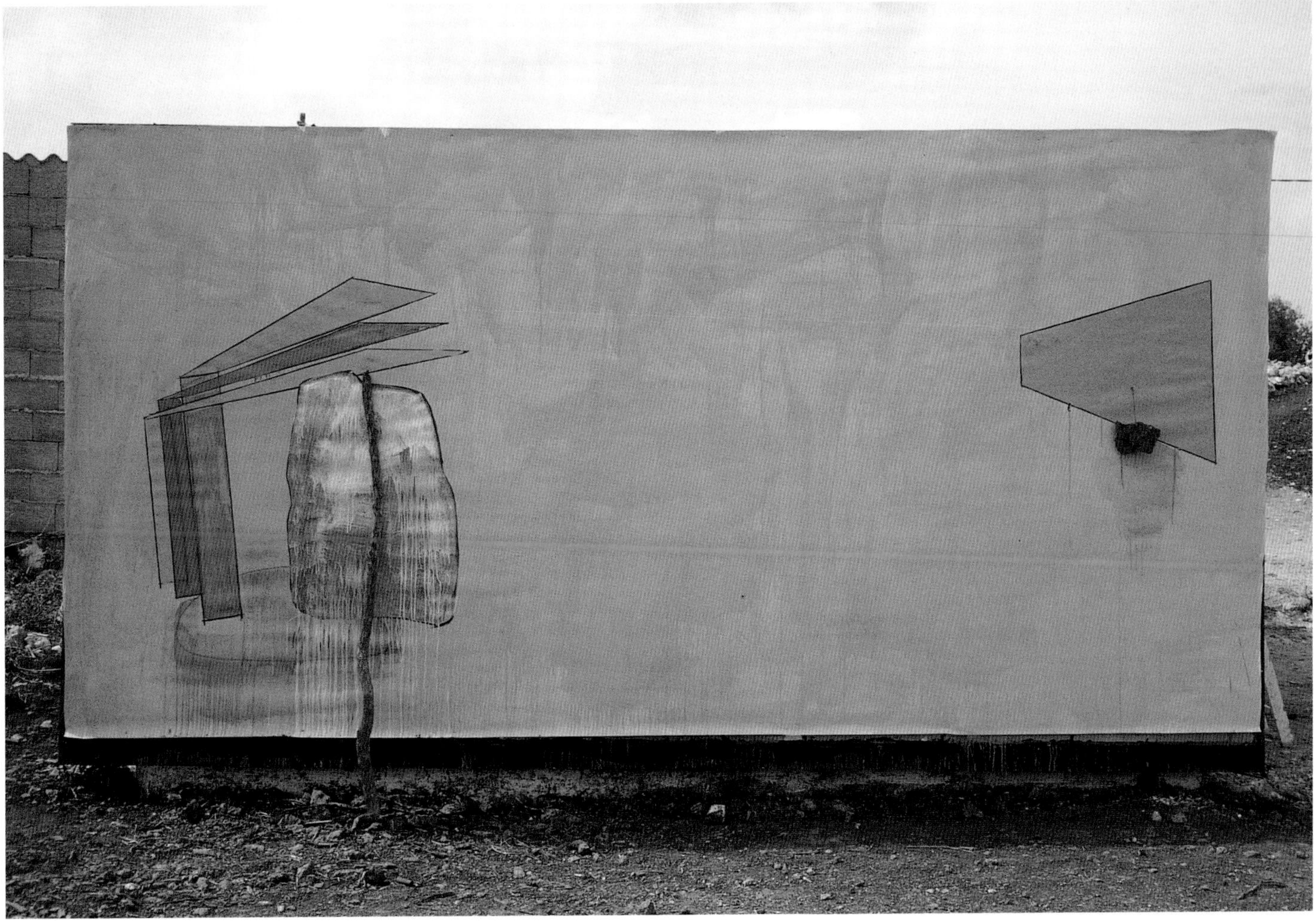

swimming pool   master bedroom   mistress bedroom   coal bunker   scullery
larder   kitchen   bathroom   shower room   sauna   jacuzzi   ha ha
flower arranging room   utility room   steam room   laundry   den   playroom
sexarium   dovcot   carp pond   conservatory   pond box room   aquarium
billiard room   pantry   plant room   library   moat room   moat
anti room   cat flap   conversation pit   patio   nursery   gallery
lounge   smoke room   snug   stable   outside mixer tap   greenhouse
gravel drive   dumb waiter   through lounge diner   serving hatch   lean too
bike shed   rabbit hutch   stable   porch   front room   hall   reception room
wet boat house   long room   balanced flue   a range   loft conversion
wine cellar   en suite bathroom   spare room   bar - b - q   a well   a folly
boot room   cocktail bar   airing cupboard   avery   bird table   gazebo
sun deck   veranda   bay window   picture window   cloak room   dressing room
car port   double garage   twin bedroom   gymnasium   tennis court
chapel   camomile lawn   herb garden   orchard   stream   lake   wood

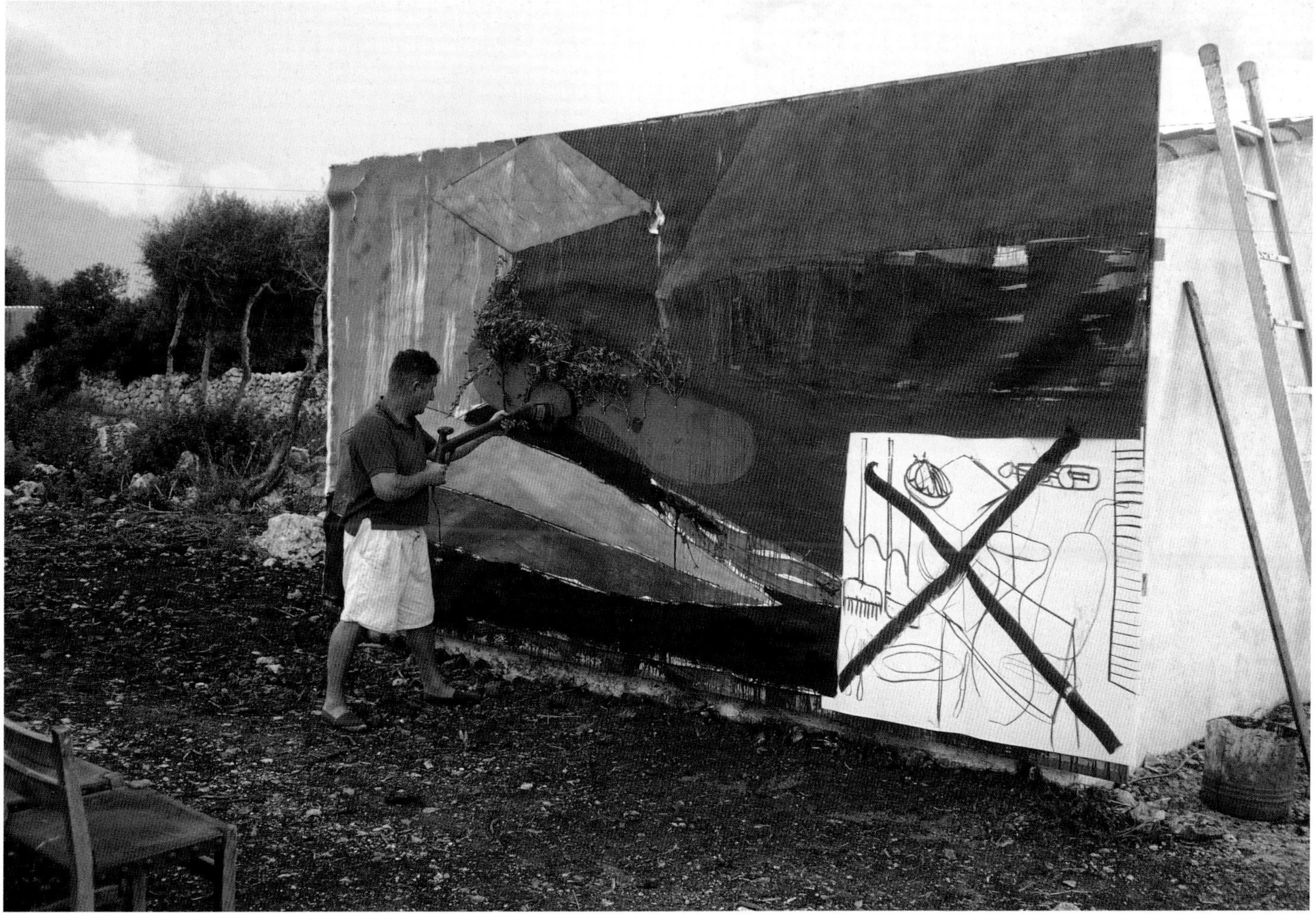

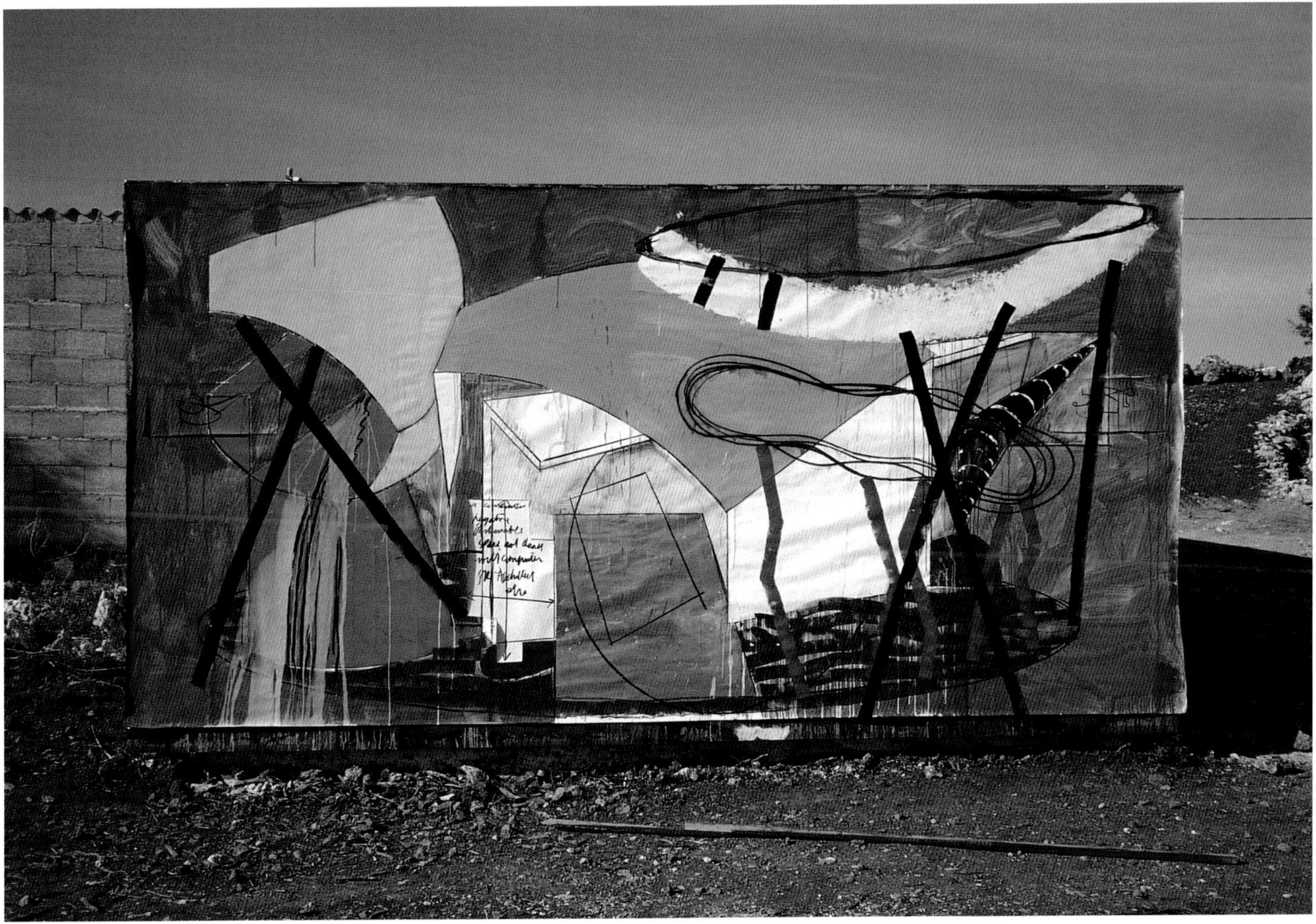

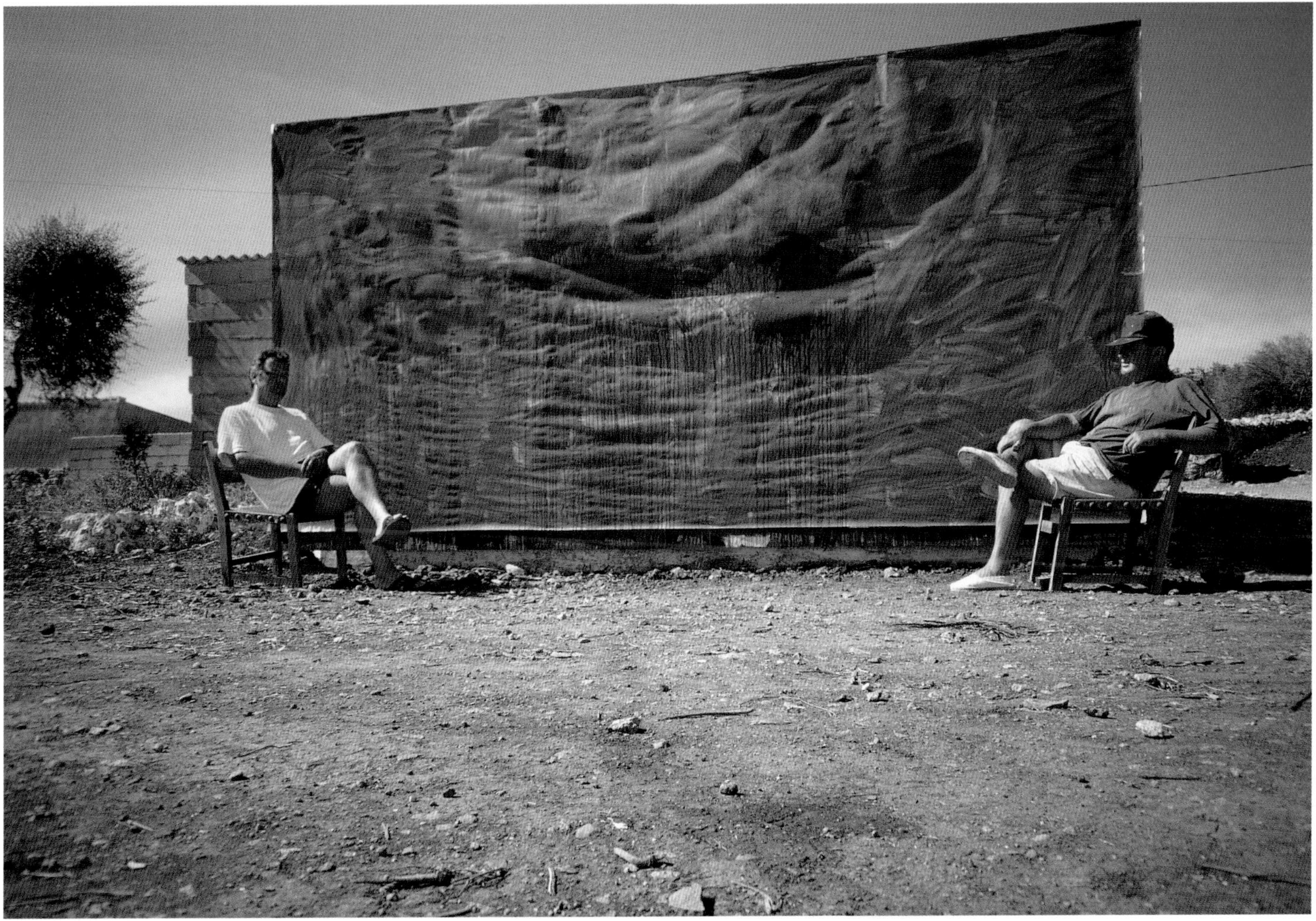

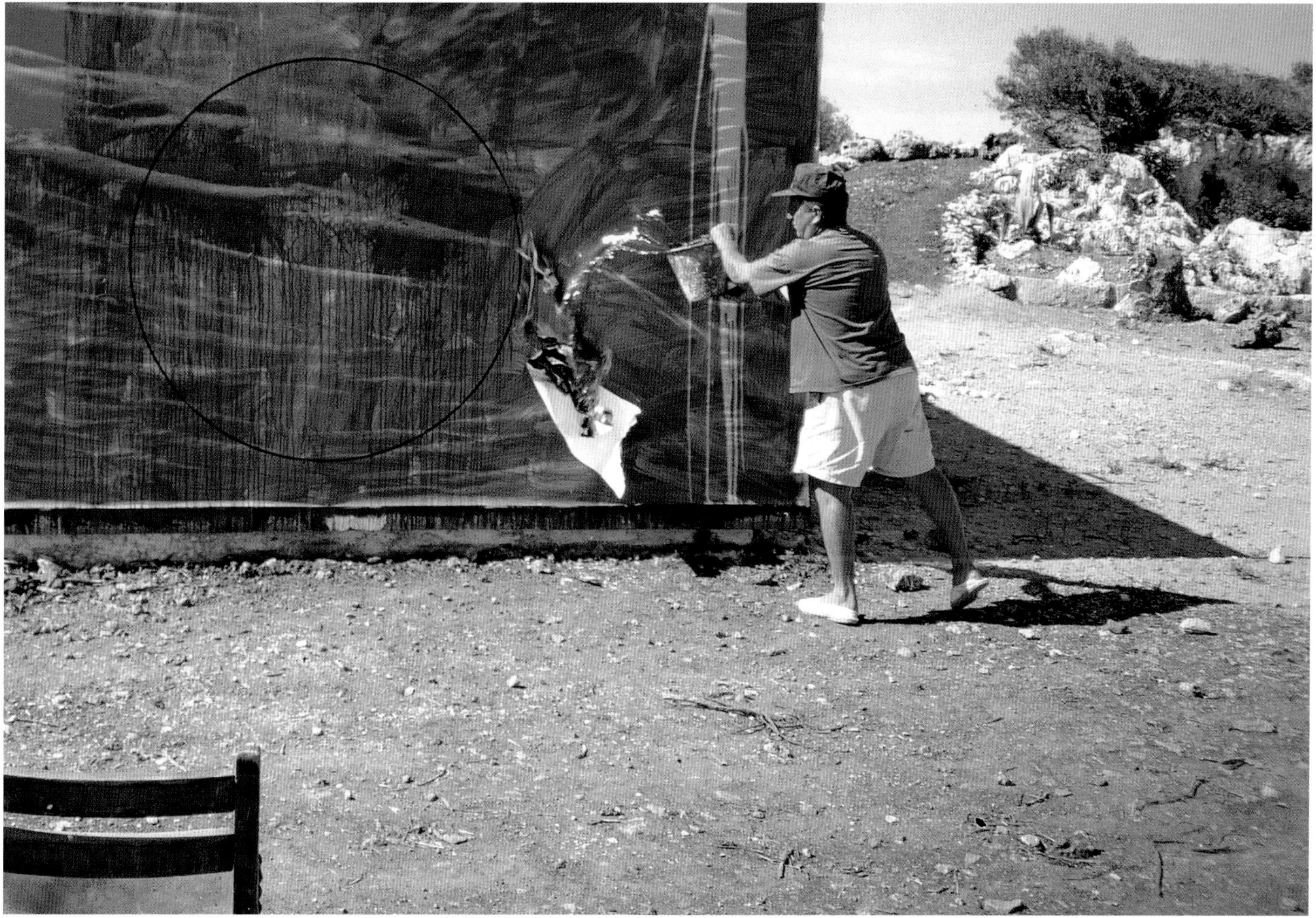

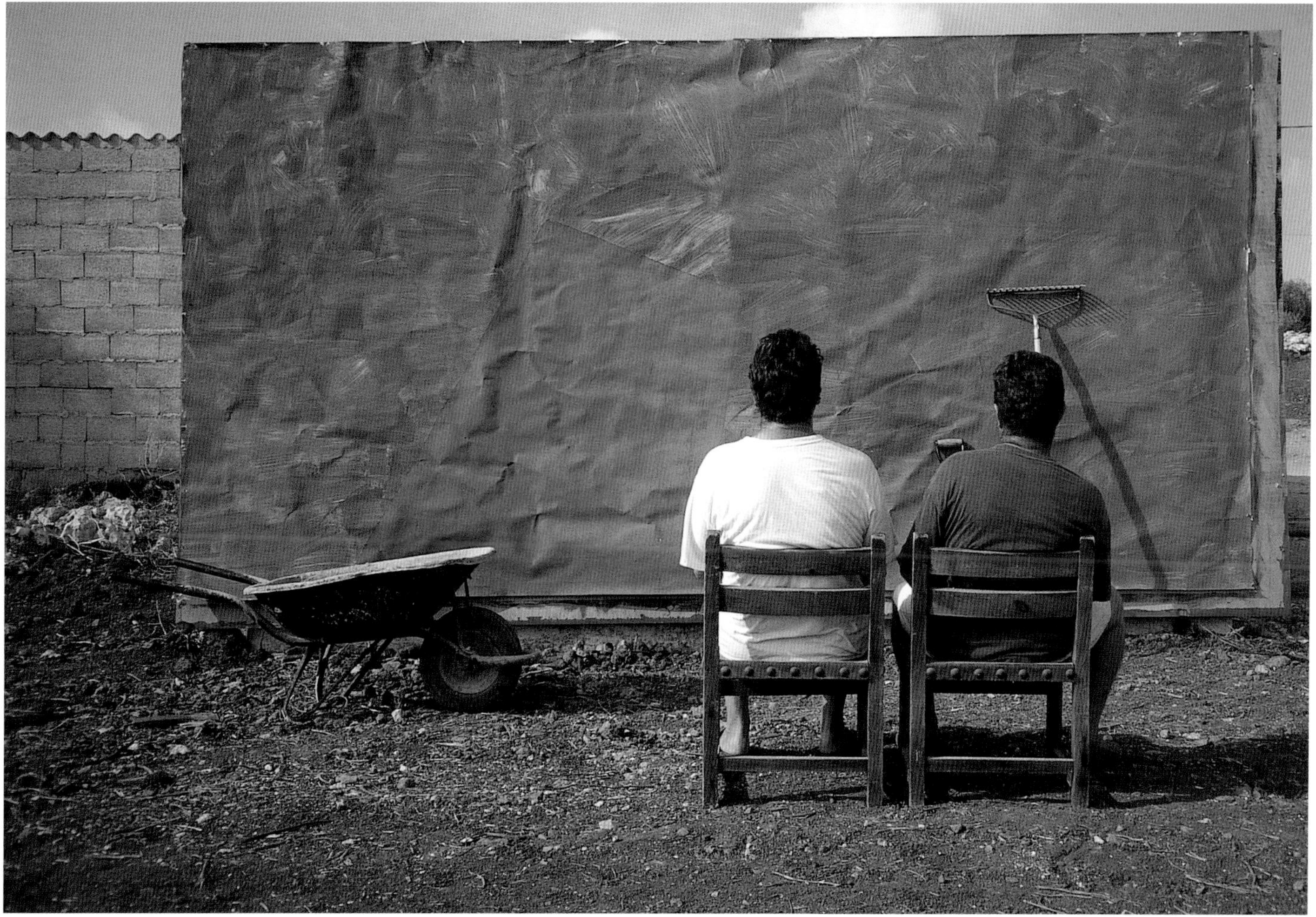

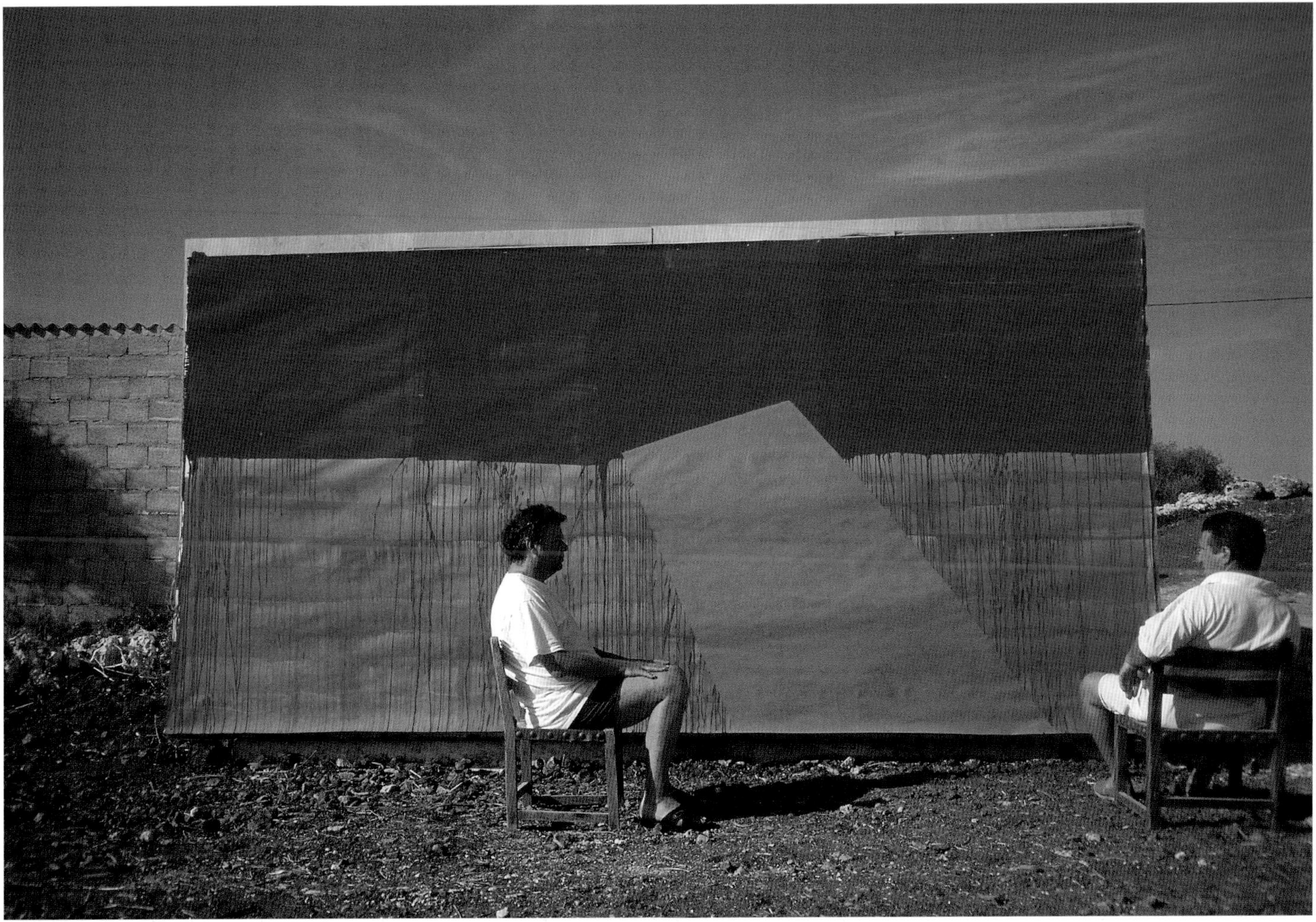

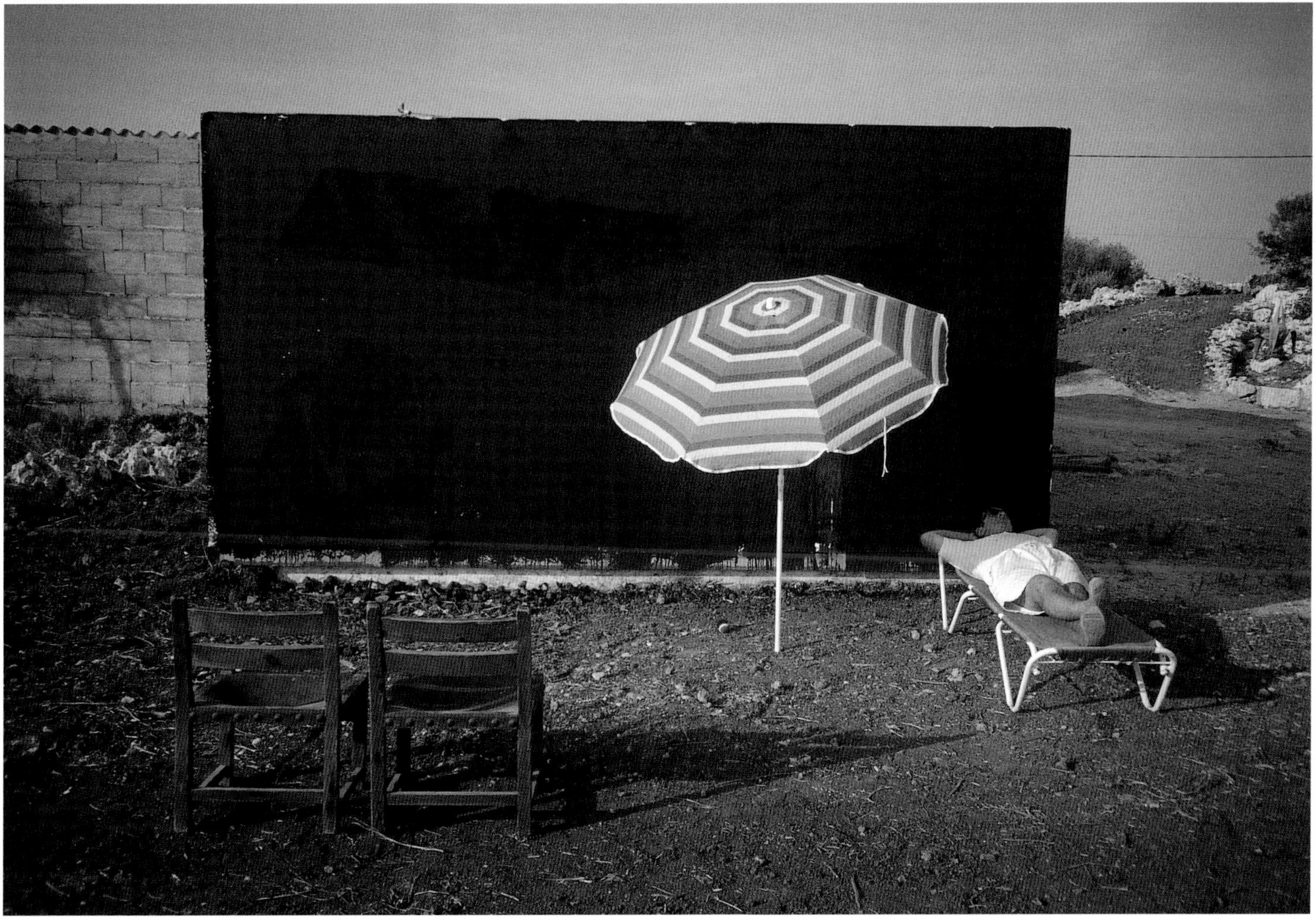

the
house
of
discomfort
is
perhaps
more
ideal
than you think

there
is
a
freedom
from
the
tyranny
of
style

a   squeaky floor is a cheap burglar alarm
a   better future is ever present

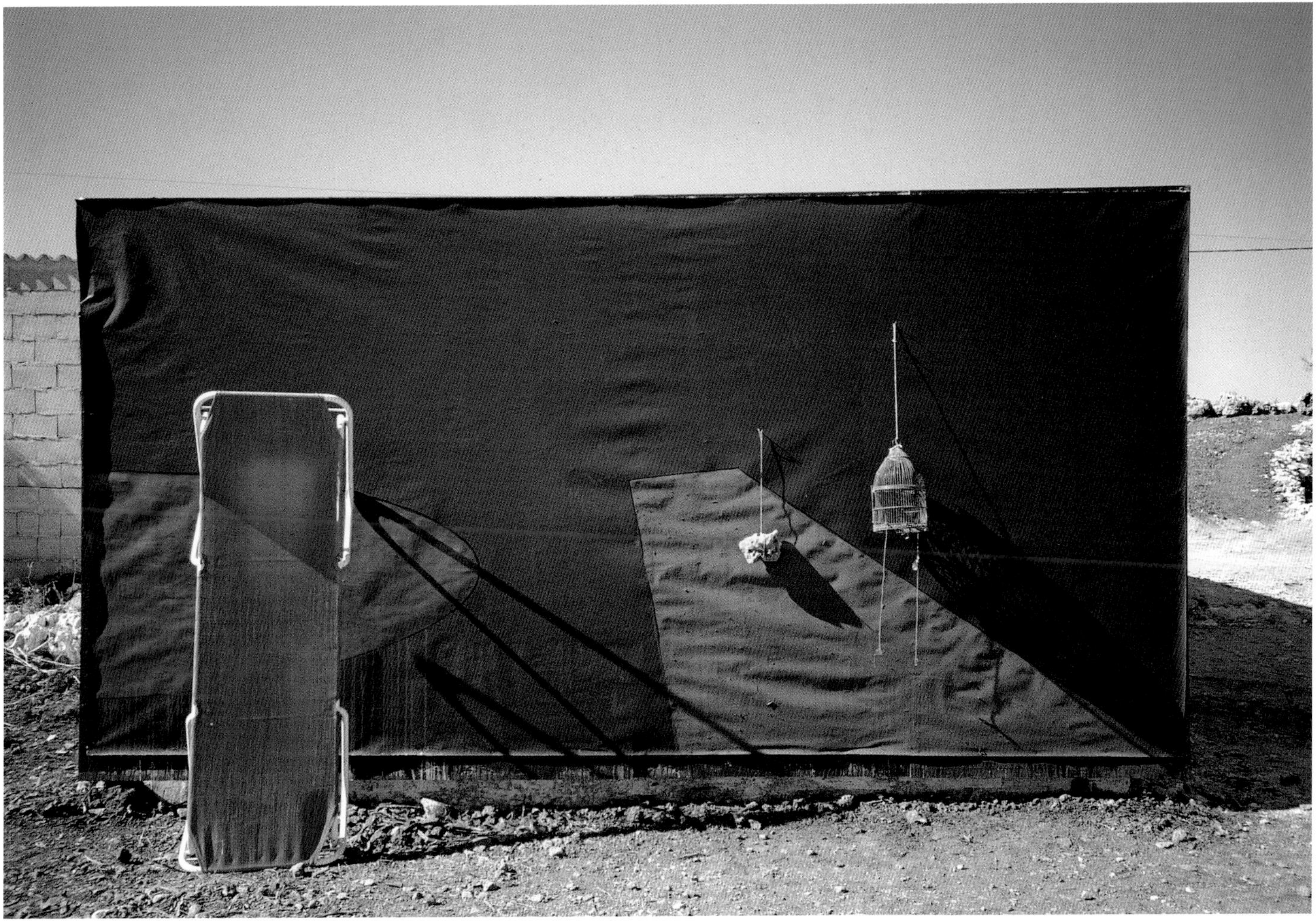

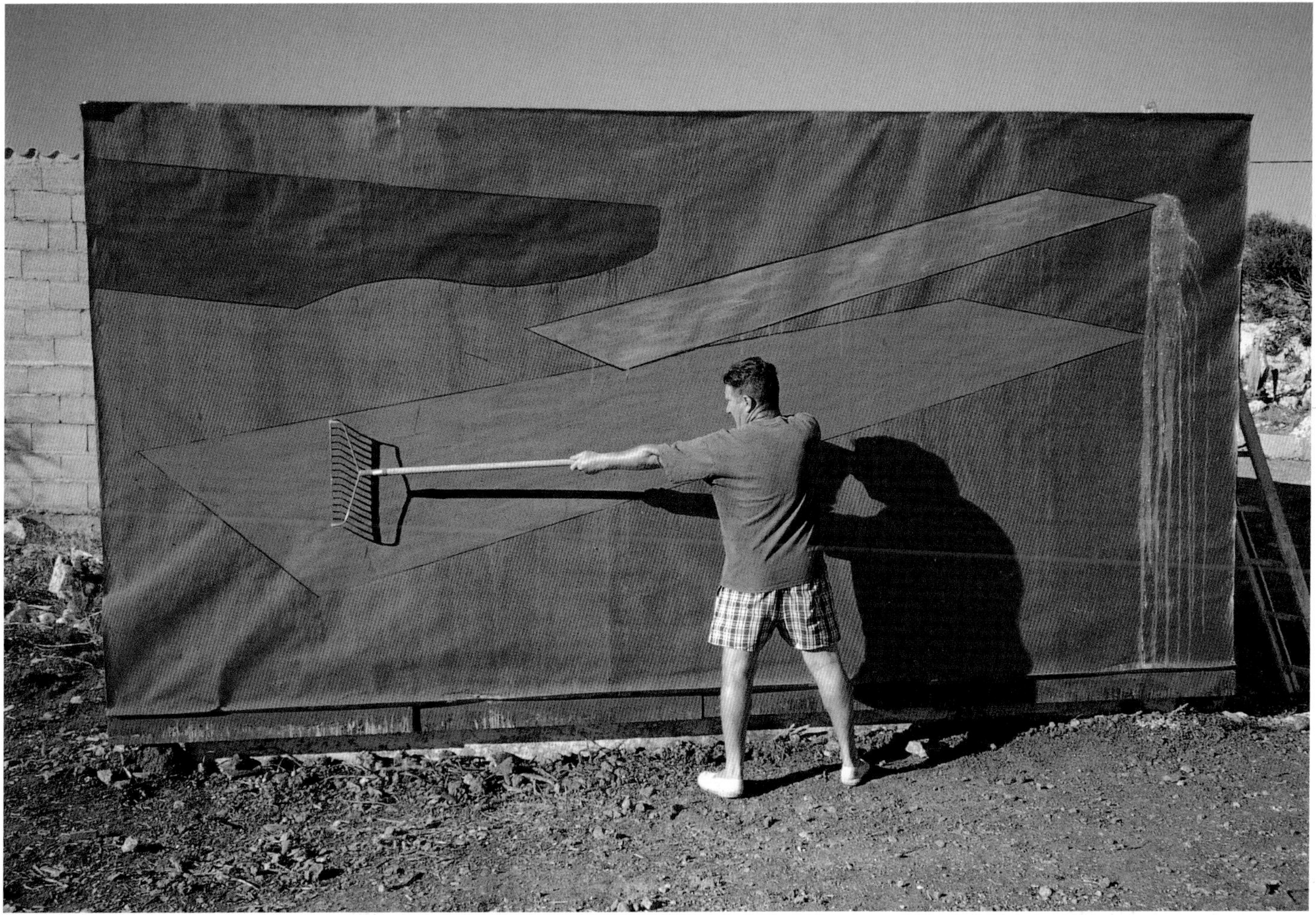

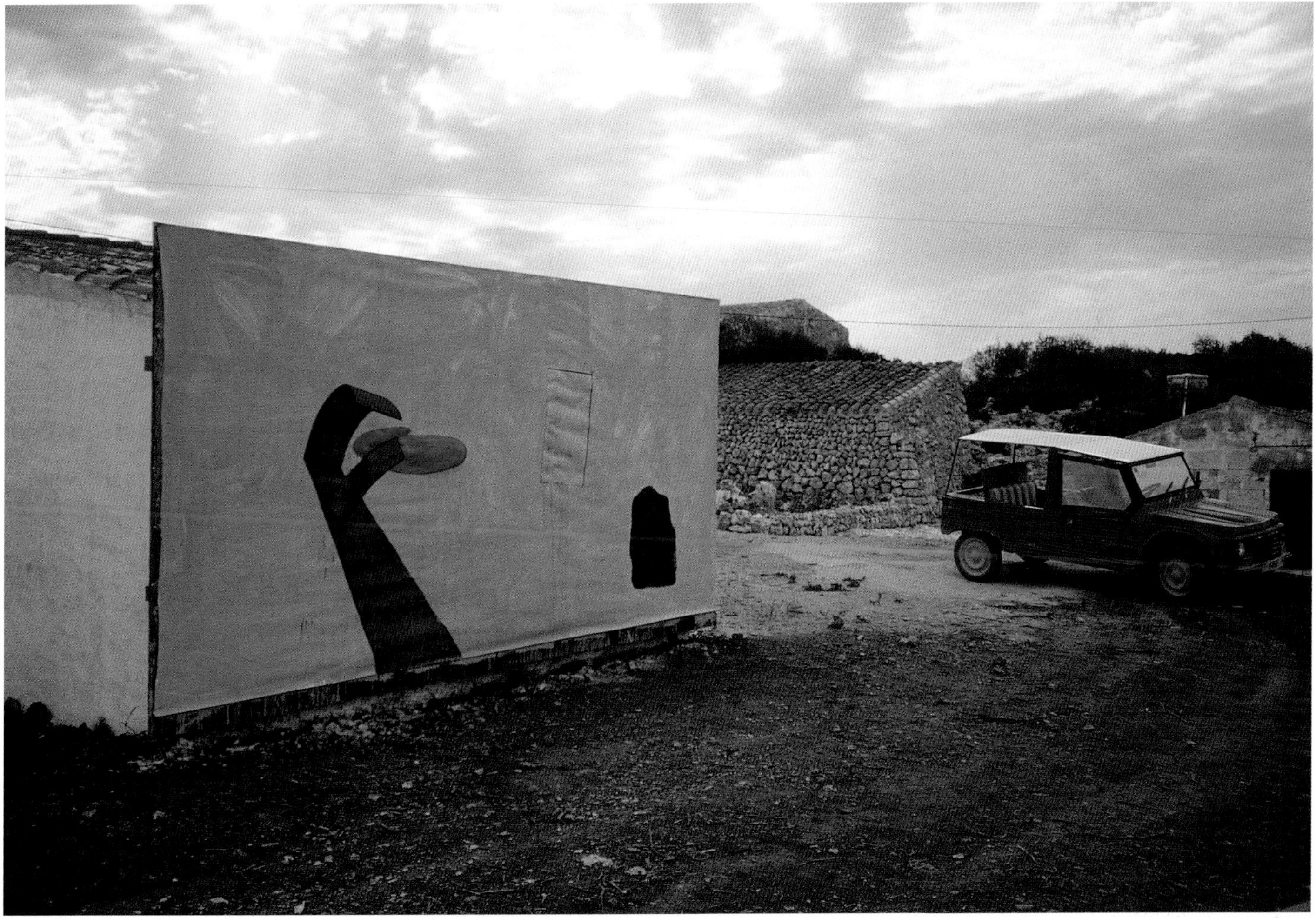

could   a   garden emerge from a weedy patch of dried scrub

could   a   work   be   discovered to sustain us through a winter

could   every   work   be   walked on

could   the   roof become a street

could   the   surface of the earth be rearranged to suit the mood or the occasion

could   flowers grow through such a shifting termoil

could   the   soil contain a beauty that would drive a new way of seeing

                                                    under the feet lie a million possibilities

          a   garden of activity

                                                    garden

a

garden of

activity

Master Bedroom

En Suite

Picture Window

Balcony

Patio

a lump of

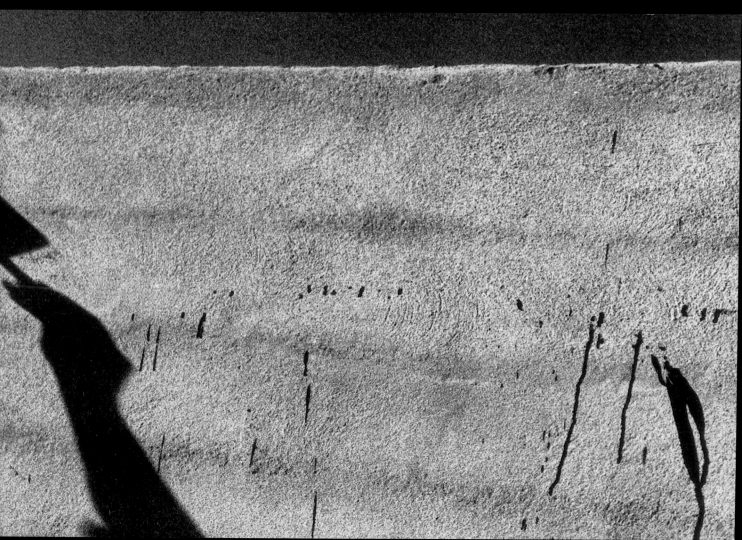

speed

still

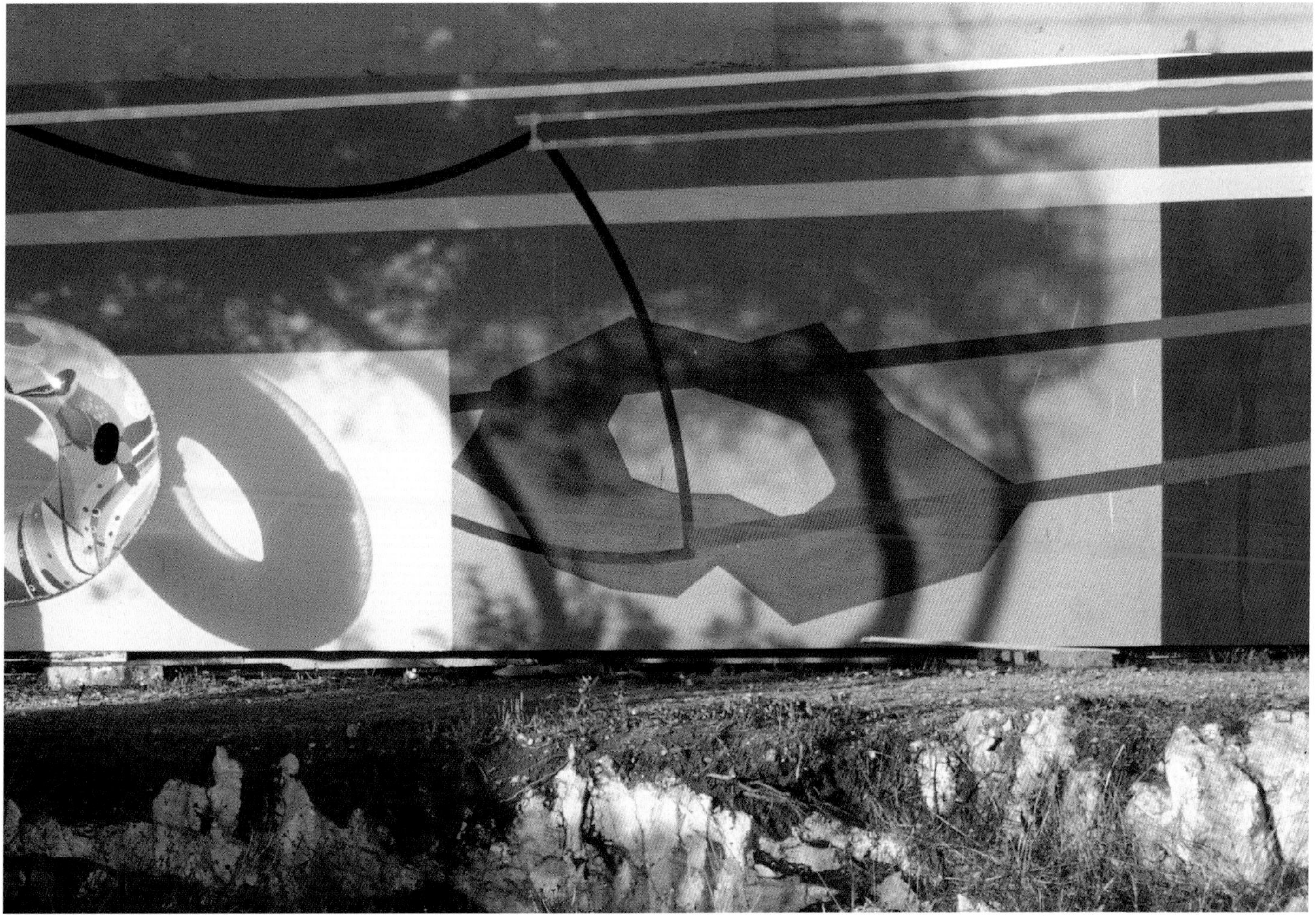

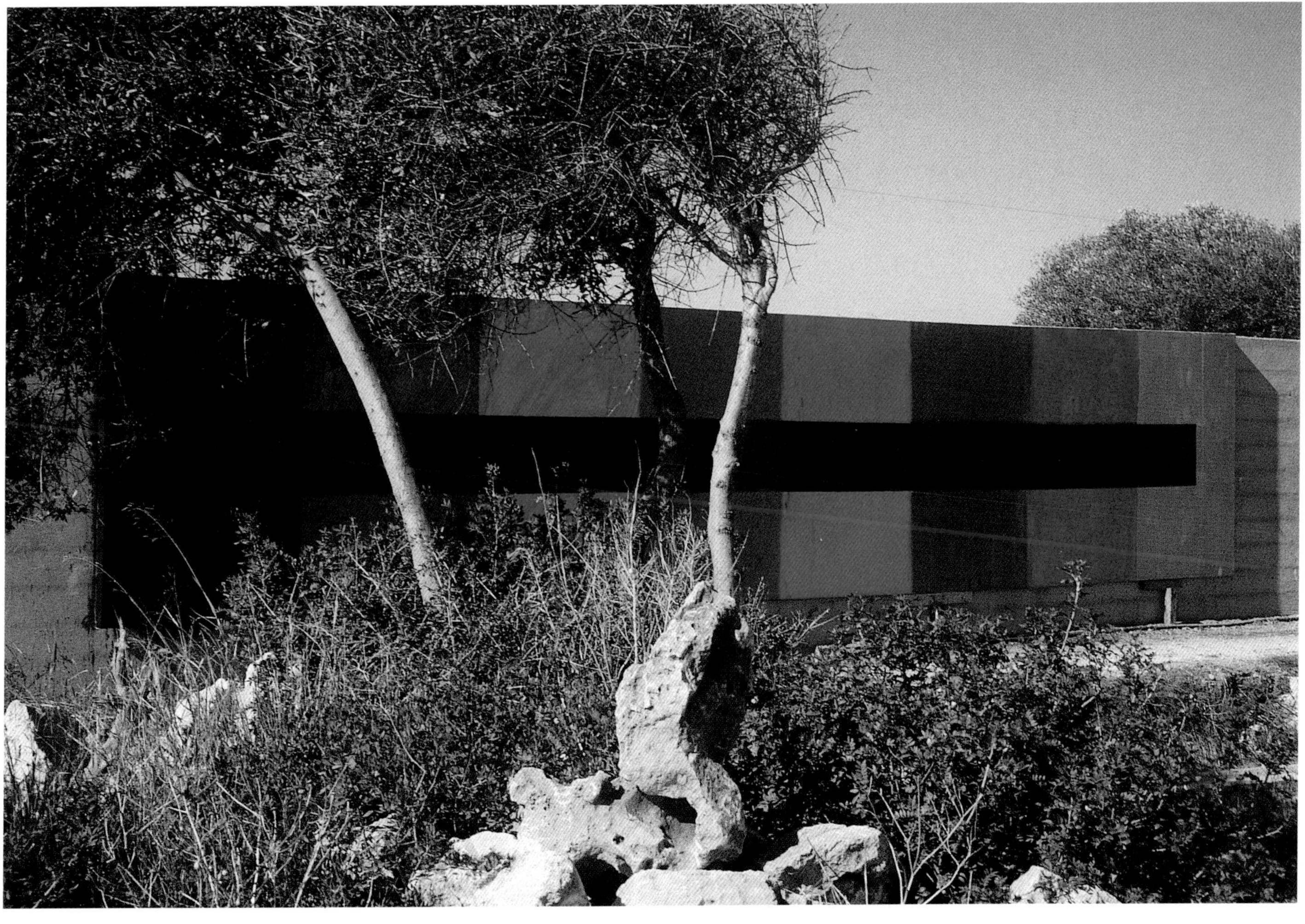

a store - house stare - house stored modern for staring at art
all art installed in store for purposes of advanced staring

gazing   glancing   glimpsing   grasping   gasping
conveyed concepts   constructions   concrete   concrete poetry
paintings prints conveyed on conveyors on multi level level art park /
car park   situation /
situations   high level   low level   eye level   mezzanine view
views   corrected perspectives   sensitive site specifics
moving installed installations   a fast ellsworth kelly   a medium paced penck
a slow rothko   some difficult judds   and an early van gogh
a big barnet newman   a seminal aoulages   a small Henry Moore
store based   store bored / score board   andre to zorio

no brick on the tate inglenook
nuek
(nuke nuke)
electric
eclectic
american influence
influenced by a mini - trip to anne hatheway's stratford - upon avon tudor patterned brick - work cottage

the venturies' inglenook lean - to national gallery extension
fire place effect and phoney academic intellectualisation brick shit - house attitudes
camouflaged in matching aquascutum raincoats
will not determine form over here

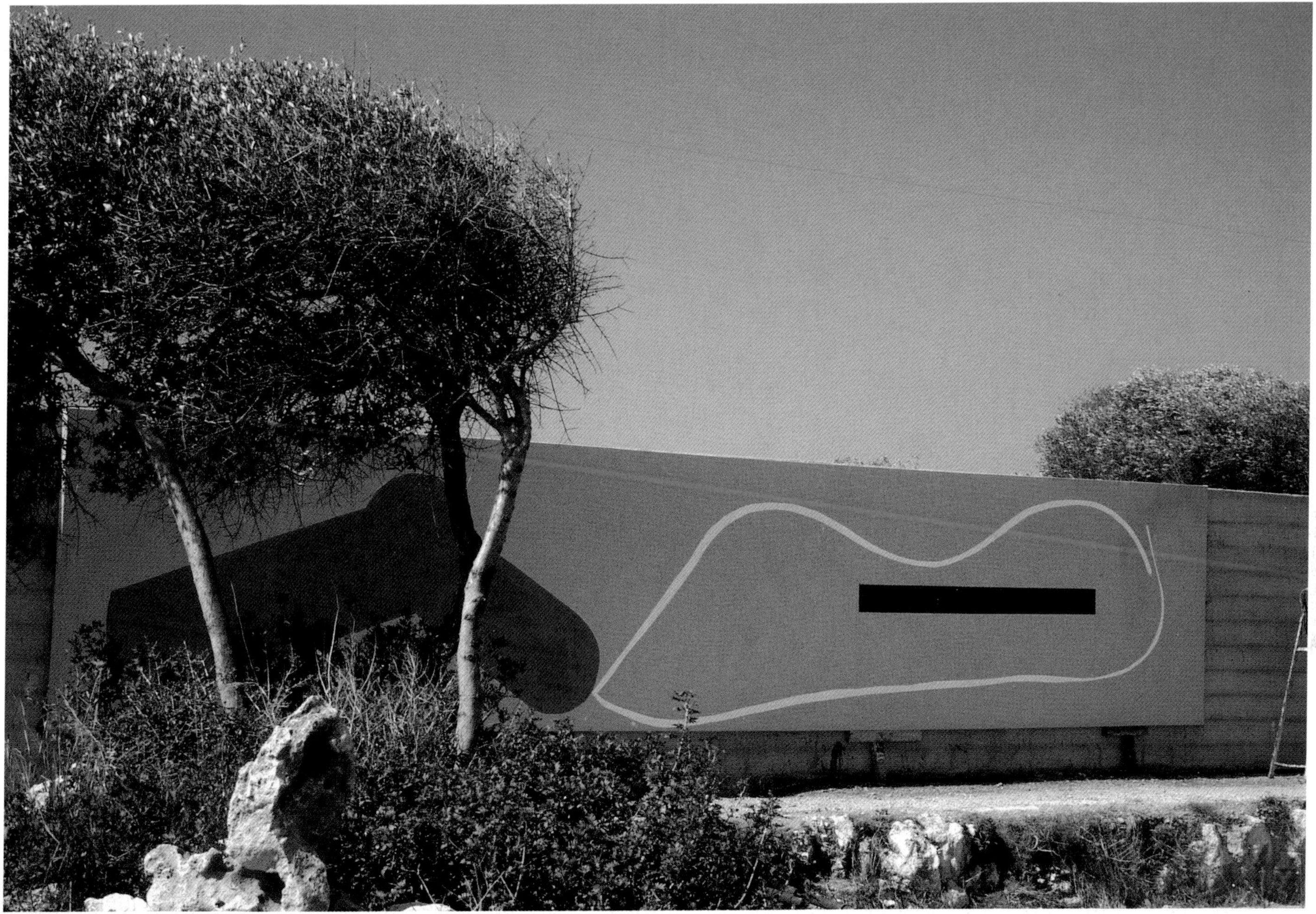

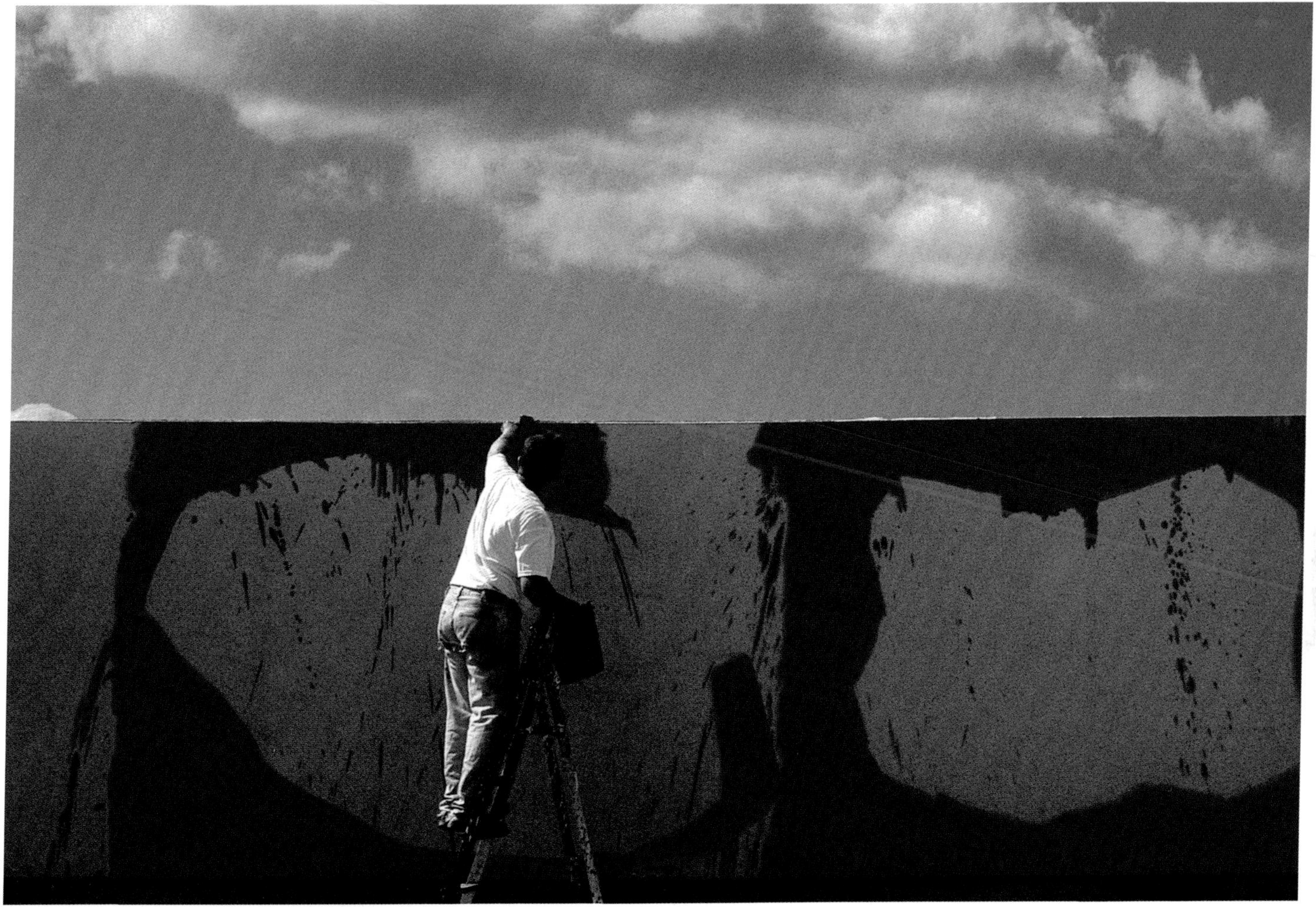

the dish of decision;   a pavilion for a parallel parliament
a place for political positions   ·   points of view   predictions   parallel poses
placements   postures   performances   and promises

parody parliament for the parody party in parallel pavilions

dish of decision not dome of division   dome of derision the dish / syndrome
no dome   no dromes   dish open dome closed system   bridge overt over it
a visual handshake
under table   tunnel vision - subvert

rome is the home of the dome   parallel debates in the dish and the dome
the dish channels it   the dome contains it

dish of desire - a transparent glass dish based on a punch bowel
a dynamic decision making dish for clear thoughts
not a cheese dish of division or administration in a dome drama dilemma

dish or dome   dome or dish   dome of discontent   dome of dullness   dish of desire
dish of delirium;   a platter parliament   a parallel parliament   nothing concealed
everything revealed   as in fireside summit handshake photo opportunities

parallel parliament   a conical gold transparent dish on a green square background
a new shape for the new government with
new thoughts   new ideas   new haircuts   new suits   old ties

a
dish

of
decision

Malagarba works. On high ground crowning the island of Menorca, I imagine Bruce and Will working in the sun of the early morning. There, in May, the earth revealed between the gorse on those hilltops still contains ruddy, moist tones, and the air is fresh with the wind-born scent of new herbs.

The buildings on this small farmstead sit compact and squat beneath their caps of tightly overlapped pantiles baked by years of sun to the earth browns of the soil. In a neatly paved yard stands a trestle table, covered by the incongruous paraphernalia of the art school: acrylic paint in squeeze bottles, brushes, markers, many pens. Two canvas seats, of the type generally characterised as 'director's chairs' sit next to it, self-consciously anticipating occupancy.

On this stage, in basic T-shirt and shorts but with colouring and physique so similar as to suggest immediately that a double act is in play, Bruce and Will apply themselves to *Sil-Opera*. It is a work on a considerable scale. A photograph of an industrial scene so drear and damply metallic as could only be located in Northern Europe has been blown up to epic size and stretched on a frame. Assiduously, the two men are applying sightlines and towering silhouettes, perfectly elliptical clouds and orange trumpets to the image. The building, a Rotterdam grain silo, appears convulsed by an orgy of transformation. The effect is dynamic, suggesting not only new forms but also sounds, movements, spheres of activity.

Work stops, momentarily. The northern scene in its new environment sits absorbing the colour, absurdity and warmth of the south. In drying, the colours are taking hold in the hardening light with a plausible permanency. Though unfinished, the image is photographed in this incarnation. It is almost time for lunch.

Conversations. Bruce McLean and Will Alsop have conducted a happy dialogue, on and off, for twenty years. Both have independent careers, but come together on these occasions for an exchange of words, shape and colour, giving rise to multi-layered works without any required point of reference or accountability in their creation.

When they met for the first time in the bar at the Riverside studios where both were working in 1979, it was the beginning of a working partnership of rare quality. Will, with clear memories of his parents' bridge habits, wanted to establish a weekly soirée that would synthesise talk, drink, paint and performance.

The Alsop/McLean bridge circle took place once a week at Bruce's new studio in Park Royal. The outcome was often unexpected, always unusual. Works created there could relate to projects that either was working on at the time, though both always resisted closing off opportunities by any direct reference. Instead these essays – paint, sculpture, the odd performance – remained oblique and adventurous.

When Bruce bought the farmhouse in Menorca, a regular pattern of creation could flower.
A spirit of unconscious behaviour pervades all that is done at Malagarba.

Not finishing remains a central concern of the Alsop/McLean amalgam – perhaps because there is no commission, no deadline, no reason. Some shining facet or shard will emerge from these labours in the hot sun, but indirectly. Then, in a moment of recognition, a shadow fall or interplay of shapes will suggest itself to either artist as they labour in deep autumn and help resolve an architectural or aesthetic dilemma.

Both are at pains to express the easy nature of this, an organic collaboration. There is little argument that comes uninvited and no discontent, both released as they are from the nagging of patron, critic and client. That they are creatively unbridled is suggested by the scale and sweep of these large works. But this is serious play – a bounty of space and materials is used to full advantage as architect and artist work in the creation of... what, exactly?

The Canvas Became the Ground on which We Stood. Is this landscape art? The format chosen is almost a camp amplification of the traditional landscape. The titles and subjects often deal ostensibly with a real location or topographical brief. Nevertheless, as is the manner with landscapes, the works leave behind real or idealised places for the diorama of the dream. Released by imagination to explore the vistas and clear air of Malagarba, they start to elude the prescriptive canvas. This may begin with the inclusion of a dining chair, nailed to the board as the tail finds the donkey in the children's game. Or protrusions are added at right angles, catching the lengthening shadows of these peerless evenings.

With due assistance, sometimes works are discovered at great remove from the main theatre of activity. Large, irregular pieces of canvas are found lying in fields as if in abortive escape, felled in a bid for freedom.

The farm, with the tiered hillside beyond, turns out to be a receptive context. The vision spreads into the view like ink on a blotter. If Park Royal confounded the notion that it is environment that begets creative life, perhaps, after all, the contrary is true. The space, the unbridled sky, the absence of specifics in the vista prove spurs to expansive modes of expression. Mirrors placed on the stage catch the view. The artistic foil is uppermost.

Bruce and Will continue in their restlessness. A plane of colour is altered by a perpendicular challenge in a contrasting hue. Moments of craft are encountered in an atmosphere of flux. Works are caught intermittently in the shutter of the camera, to shift again as the chair is removed once more, or to include a denuded bush petrified in its first maturity, or even the changing position of a shadow. The work of the morning, seemingly so robust, submits to impermanency. Those acres of colour, those vast tracts of flat paint dominate, but from them shapes and forms begin to assert themselves, leaving the canvas, breaking out into the landscape.

Event supplants *landscape,* the idle picturesque fragmented by dynamic, contrary forces.

The Ideal Home. Sometimes the architectural influence is palpable. The proposed forms of a new Potzdammerplatz for Berlin are the subject of an early series of paintings, for instance, and the manifestation of the stage in 2002 evokes the tabletop proposition of several Alsop building projects. However, these works satisfy beyond an interpretation as architectural anguish or theorem.

Malagarba posits spontaneity as its key tenet. Bruce identifies the conventional architectural role as that of the *auteur* who waits to be asked. The mark of the professional is indelibly stamped on him. The artist on the other hand does not have an option to be professional retained. His role is to deliver from the soapbox though no audience may have gathered.

For Will and Bruce, architecture is to be co-opted for its insight into spatial forms and play, but it is subsumed into the broader sweep of notional human activity, thought and whimsy. If either holds a philosophy, or for that matter if they share one, it could be contained in that favourite aphorism...

City as Opera. Why, they ask, are cities so crushing, so confining? Alsop and McLean incite the statements of arrival, of departure. Create places for beautiful clothes to be worn, luxury cars to be driven down broad boulevards, entrances to be made on steaming trains disgorging jewelled travellers on to bright red carpets. Excess is everyone's prerogative. What are they for, these coveted designer dresses or automobiles designed by fighter pilots if they have no suitable context, no backdrop of sufficient flair? *La Traviata* does not work without its gilded salons, nor *Tosca* with no battlements. What are we to make of our surroundings if they do not incite us to extreme behaviour? So it is human actions – mischievous, sensible, sad, elated – that are suggested by the moment of the canvas; the impermanence and transition form part of the pattern.

At Malagarba priorities shift and fuse. A party on the platform becomes the singular statement of the week's work.

The Stage. Costume rears its head. Once more we are in the realm of performance. With the creation of the stage, we return to the arena of Bruce and Will's first collaboration, when Will designed the costumes for Bruce's opera, *the masterwork of the awardwinning fishknife*. So, in 2002, Miss Nancy Alsop takes the platform in an engaging cardboard tutu and orange brassiere, constructed and made that day by Flora McLean. The stage is a device which acknowledges and promotes the tendency to contrary behaviour shown by both.

Malagarba Unbound. The camera performs its own sorcery. Photography forms a periodic intervention in the casual order of the day. Shooting the works, in close-up or at some remove, contextualises the labours of the morning in time and setting. Such is photography's commonplace: eternity in an instant. Now the farm takes its place in the frame; no longer a wall, a backdrop, but the enveloping view. Landscape and time encroach, asserting their influence.

Once the work is captured, in its moment, then come the opportunities for further manipulation. The holiday *oeuvre* is taken by Will and manipulated using the computer: adding, subtracting, evolving wild forms that spin from the flattened snapshots. It is activity further modulating the patterns of collaboration, computer play overlaying brushstroke. The sessions at Malagarba echo in the broader imagination.

"For art comes to you proposing frankly to give nothing but the highest quality to your moments as they pass, and simply for those moments' sake." Walter Pater, Conclusion to *The Renaissance*, 1868

James Hulme, October 2002

Prof. Bruce McLean has blazed an astonishing artistic career since

graduating from St Martins School of Art in 1966. His ideas are fuelled by certain obsessions: the artist in society, nuances of human behaviour, humour, class, culture, education and the right of the artist to act as foil to all these subjects. These thoughts have been worked through in multiple areas of practice: performance, sculpture, ceramics, painting, drawings, printmaking, filmmaking and architecture. He approaches each medium as if newly invented, accepting no constraint until it has been tried. The son of an architect (and the father of another), he has a particular relish for projects involving art and the built environment, which has led to projects such as the conceptual model of a primary school and intervention at Lawthorn, North Ayrshire, between 1997 and 2000.

Prof. William Alsop OBE RA is one of English architecture's most

singular exponents. For twenty years he has practised a style that embraces tenets of openness, colour, local idiosyncrasy and wit. In Europe, he made a notable contribution to the *Grands Projets* of France with the Hôtel du Départment des Bouches-du-Rhône at Marseilles, while at home in London he achieved recognition with the iconographic Peckham Library, winner of the RIBA Stirling Prize 2000. He believes that architecture can truly benefit a society too long denied its aspirations, landmarks and splashes of flair. A Royal Academician and a tutor of sculpture for several years, he nurtures links between art and the built environment that take the form of community workshops and artistic collaboration.

This book is published on the occasion of the exhibition 'Bruce McLean & William Alsop, Two Chairs' at Milton Keynes Gallery from 7 December 2002 to 19 January 2003, touring to Cube, Manchester from 28 February to 24 April 2003.

With thanks to the following contributors: Pilar Madrid, Roland, Josepp Gomila i Gonyalons, Pedro Gomila Pons, Artimis Carreras Bartroli, Russel Bagley, Jose Luis Moll Jover, Flora McLean, Piers Alsop, Tim Thornton, Nancy Alsop, Mark Boyce, Tony Casalit-Salles.

Main essay by James Hulme
Design by Mark Boyce

A STATION OF ART

A DOUBLE TAKE ON THE SITU

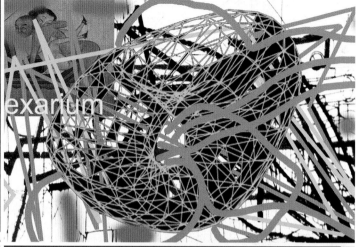

exarium

FLYING FLOWER

PAINTING FAST IN THE MIDDAY SUN CAUSES

FIRE

IS THIS ACTUA

pical lounging and longing loggia in a linear linolium loung
cent to and coming from a prawn cocktail sole bonne fem
kground in browns umbers creams off whites whi emotio
t erco... akelite bath fro and wick bedsprea
ers coming fro
groun be
erco LOOK elit

ERY FOR DOING
ON REASON
W WHAT I AM GOIN TO DO
UALLY DO IT
NEVER PREDICT.....A NEVER ENDING
PRESENT OF POSSIBILITY
EVERYTHING IS POSSIBLE...
OR IS IT.
YOU JUST HAVE TO START
THING IS WE KNOW WHEN TO

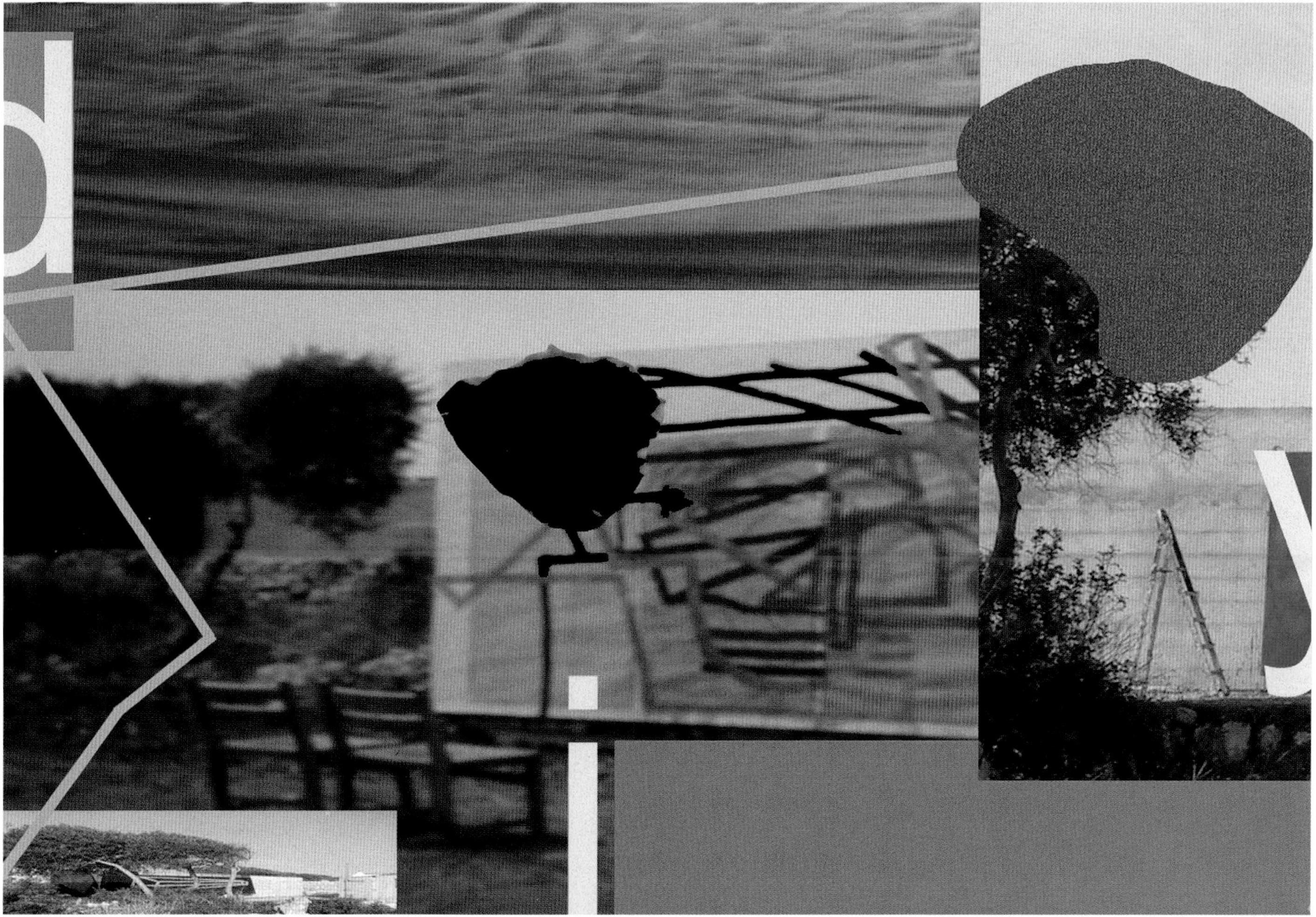
d
y

waiting

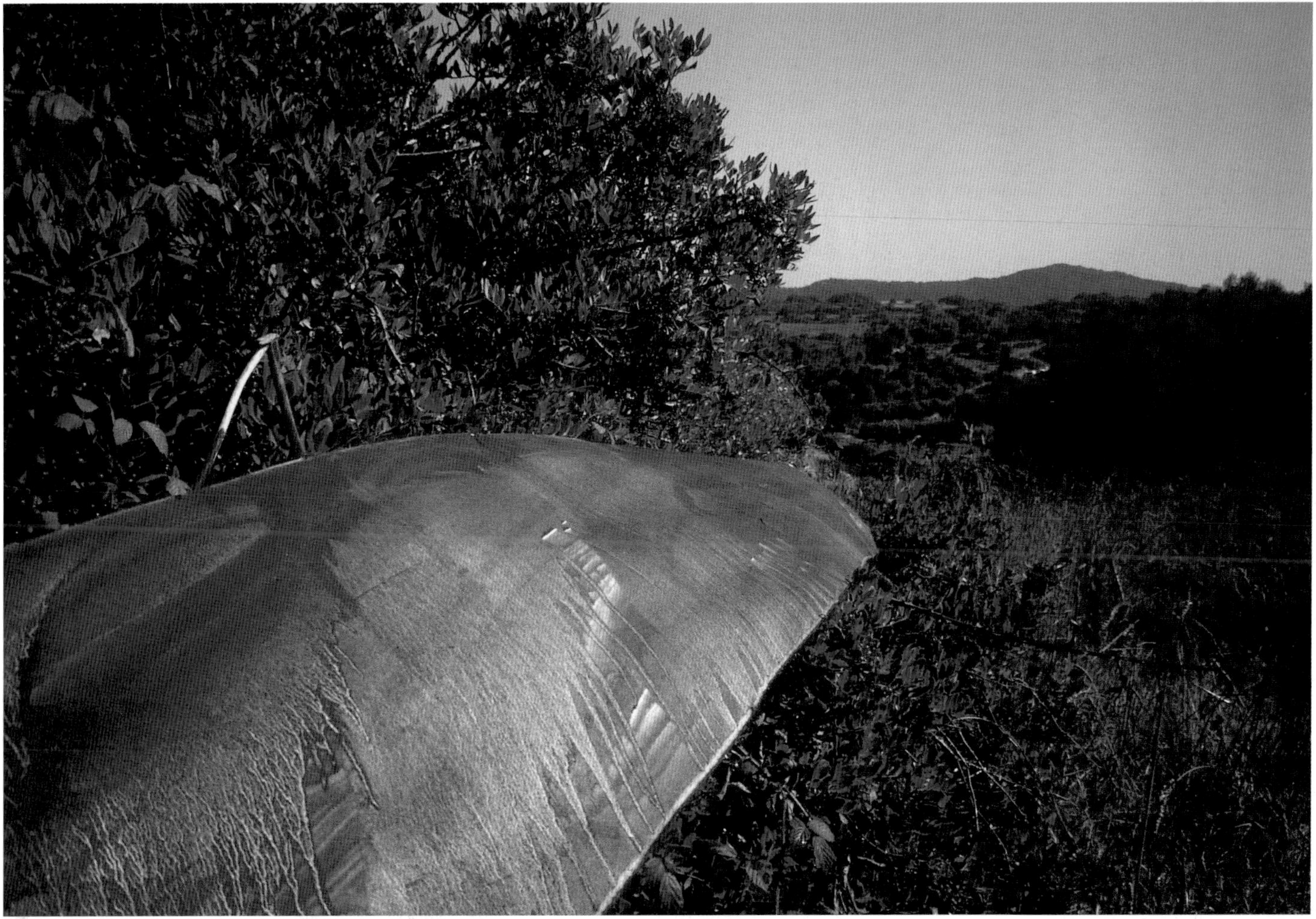

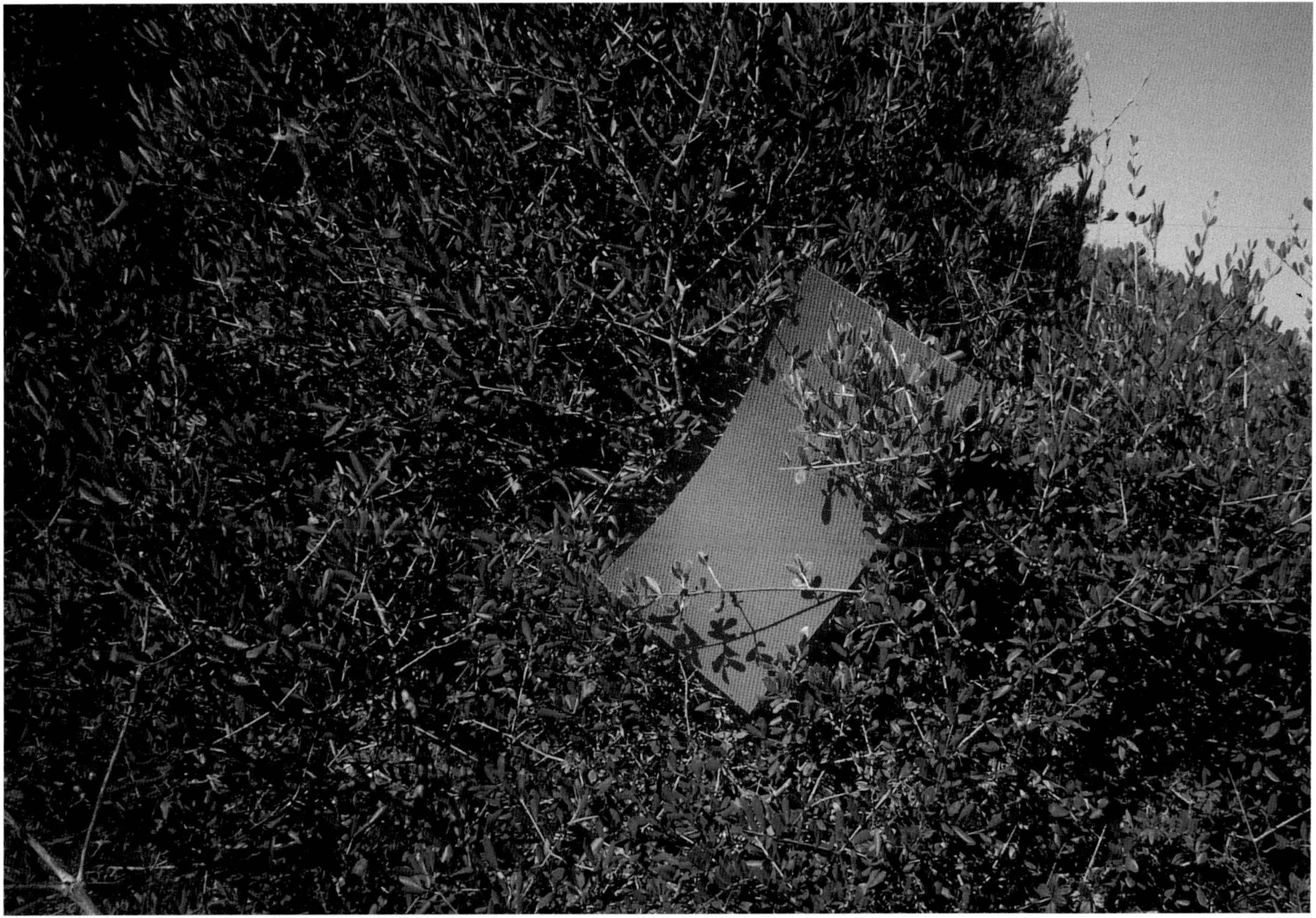

a   house of nudge
a   hall of collective   nodding
        group   nodding
                  nodding   off place
                           (shaking quaking expecting the millennium)

a   media rehearsal hall for gestural control practices
a   gestural debriefing centre:
a   building designed for the specific purpose of allowing investigations into any kind of activity gestural:
a   multi-media investigative analytical synthesising research platform theatre of research
a   general gesturing centre:
a   research project for the development of new gestural possibilities (a visual gesture bank)
a   gesture park

                        nod
                        nudge
                        wink
                        tap
                        point
                        hint
                        adumbrate
                        signal
                        shrug
                        wag
                        wave
                        gesticulate

      construction of a book on the naming of gestures
a   gesture thesaurus
      an encyclopedic nodding centre

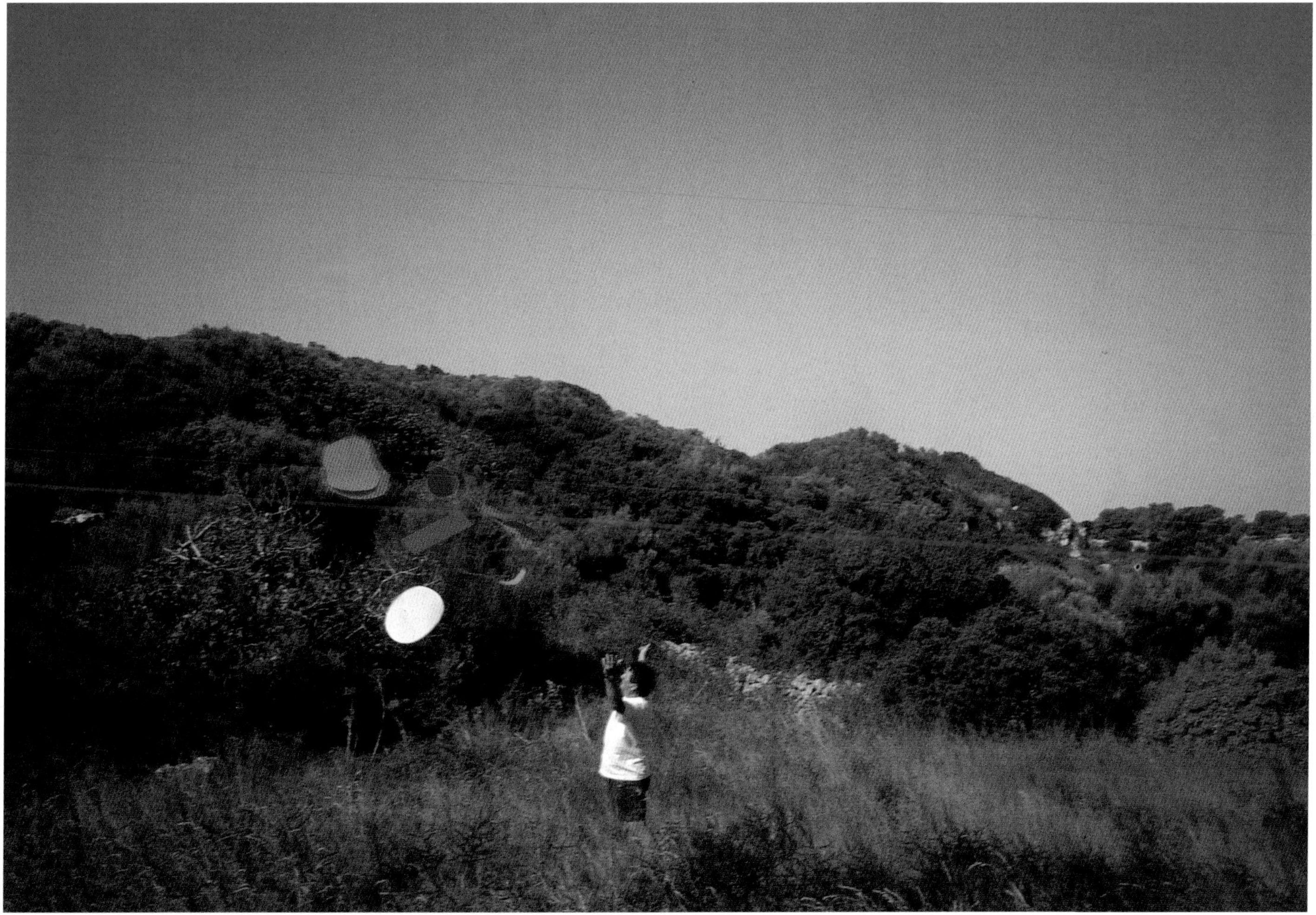

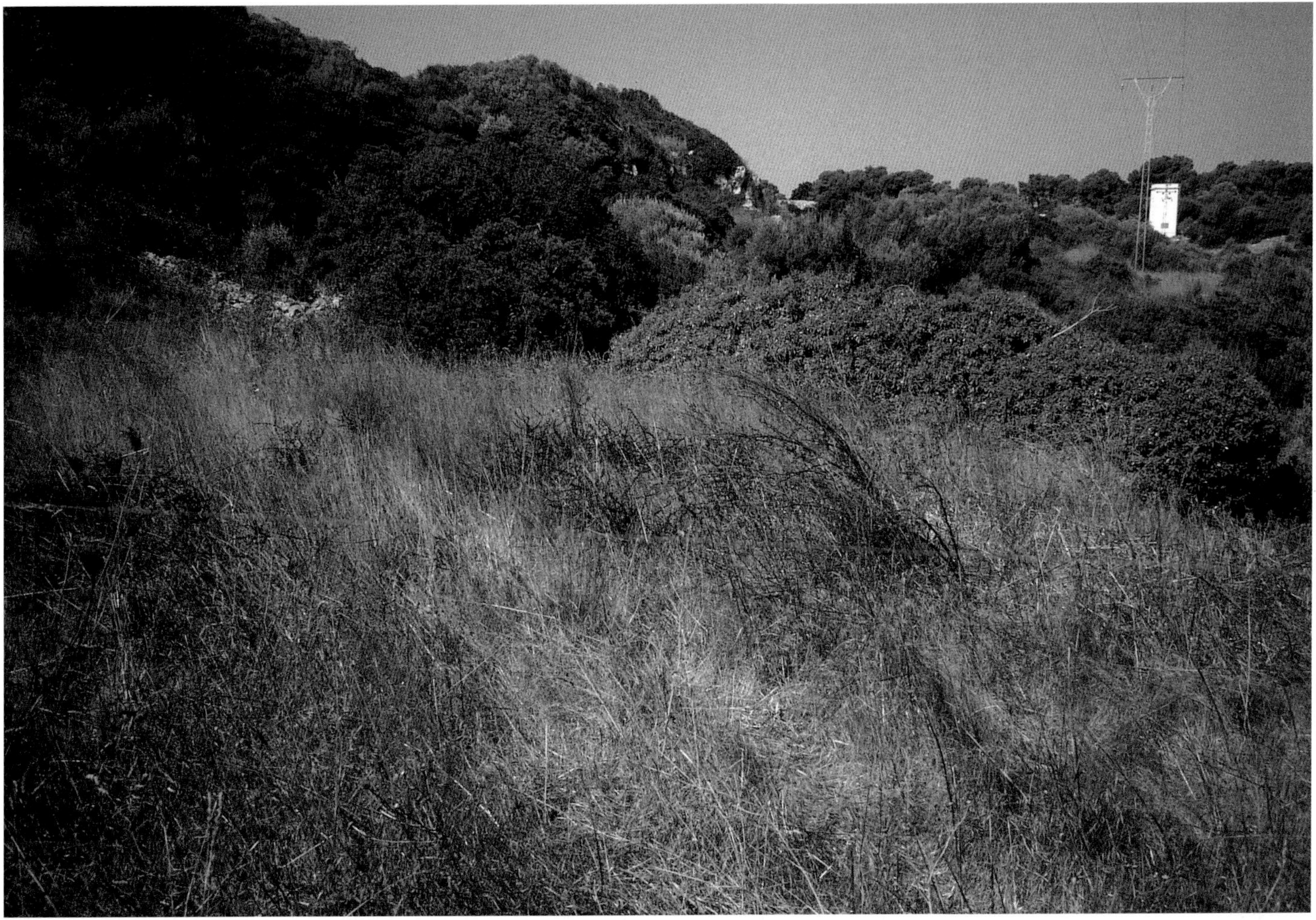

no more fast
food a look
forward to
coq au vin sole
bonne femme

brown windsor
soup rumba
bar apple
strudel and no
pot noodle

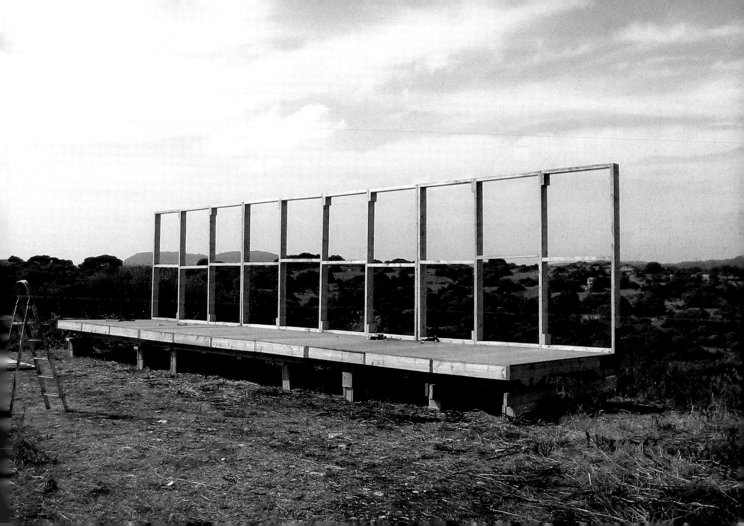

a platform
to
stage

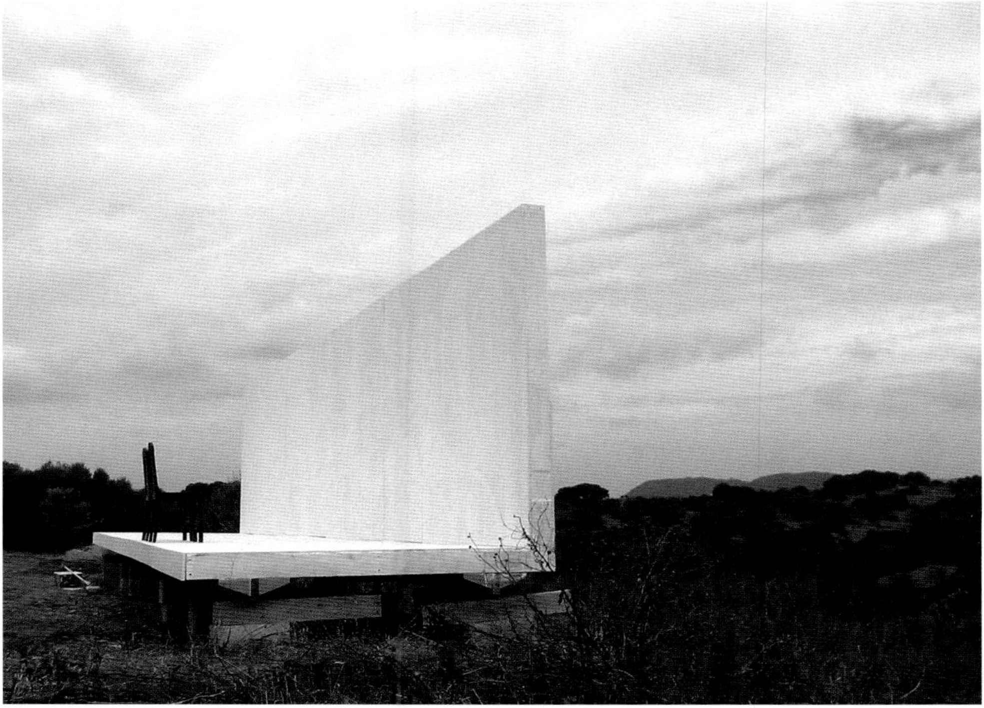

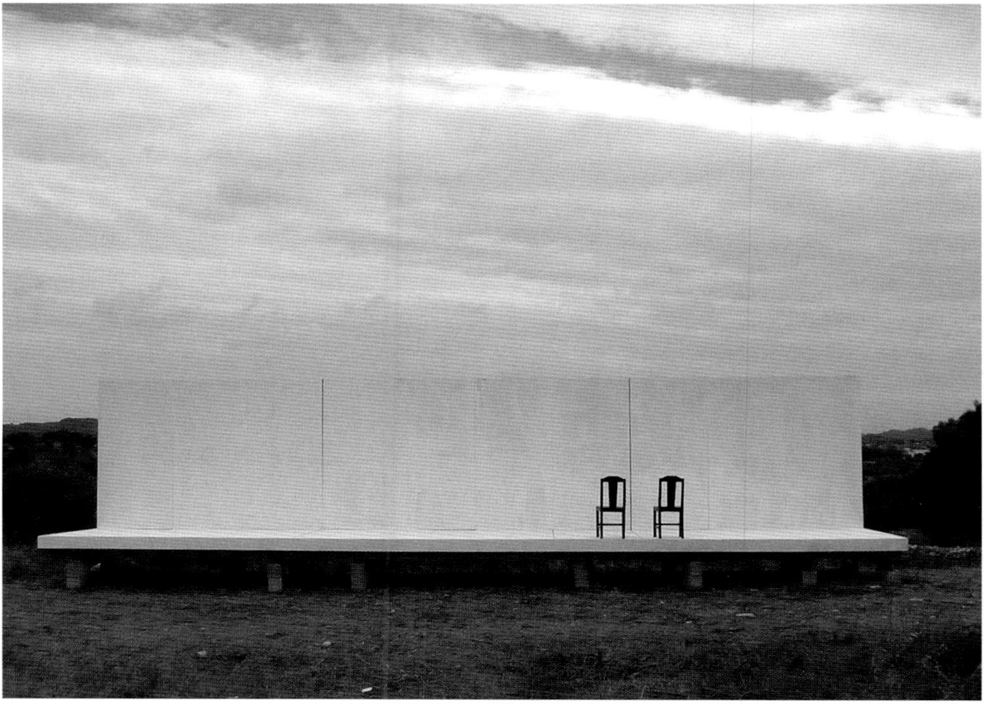

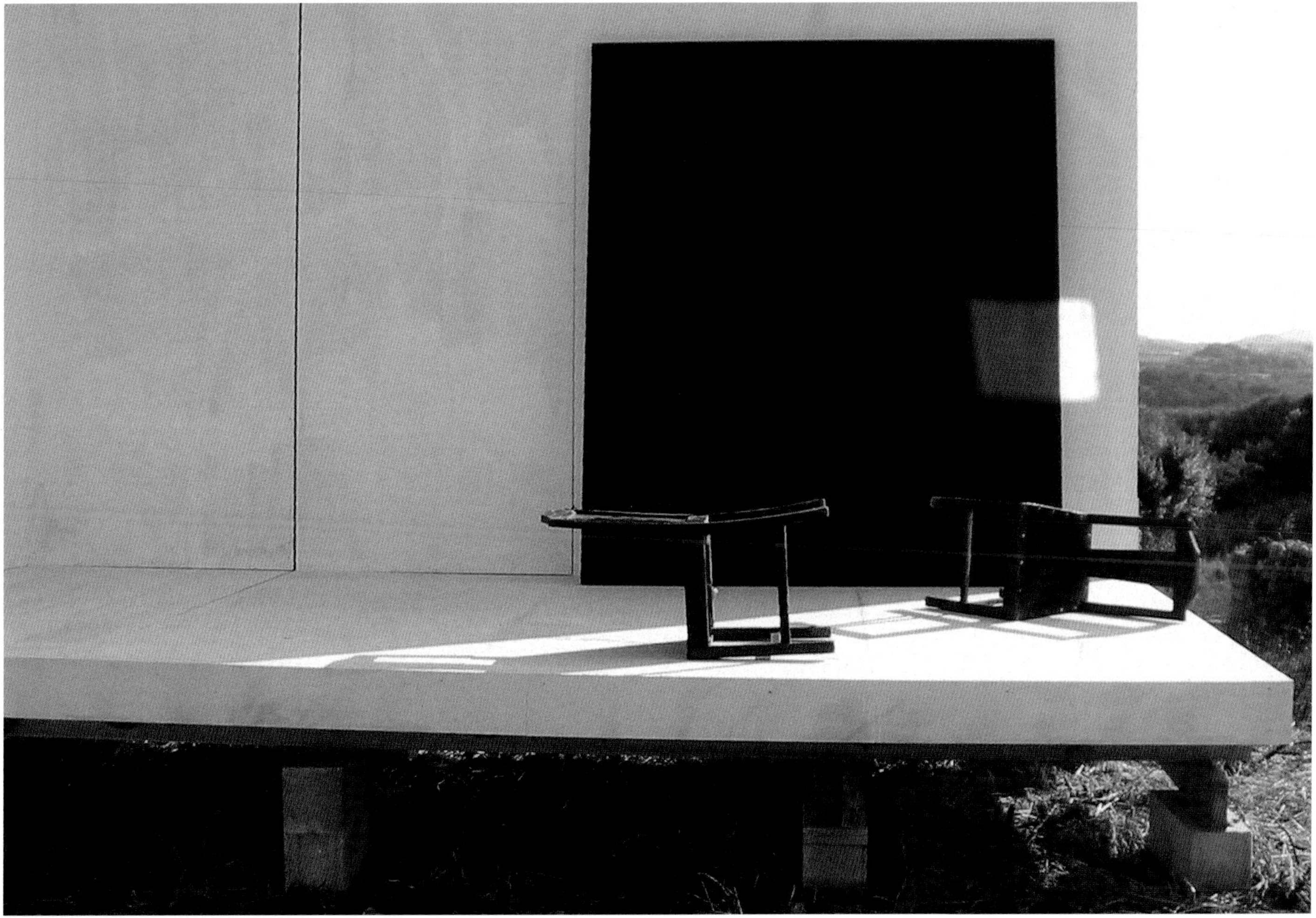

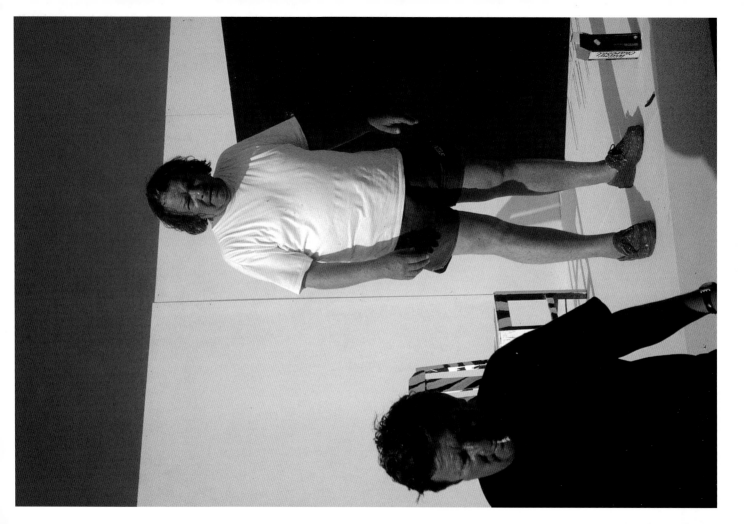

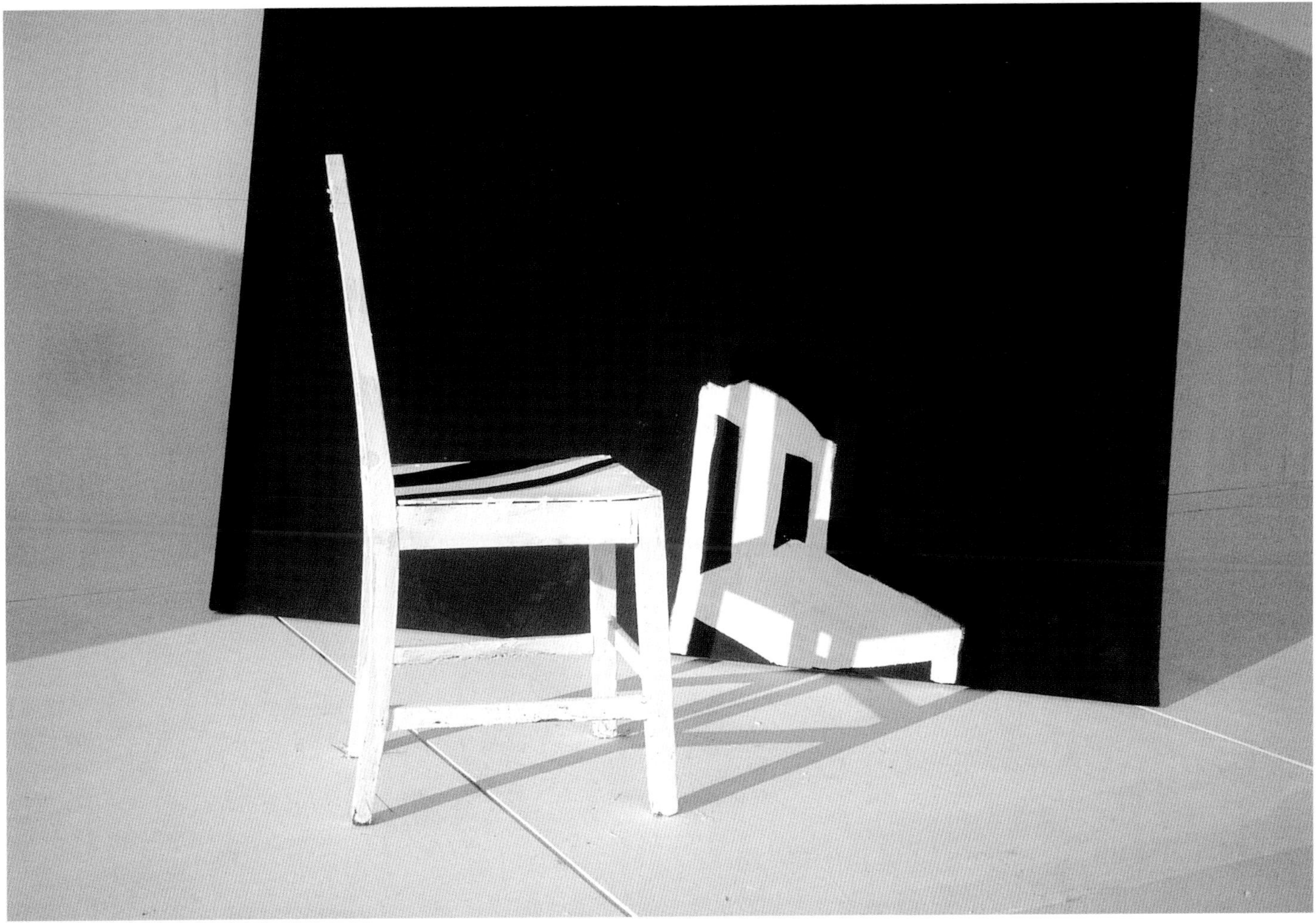

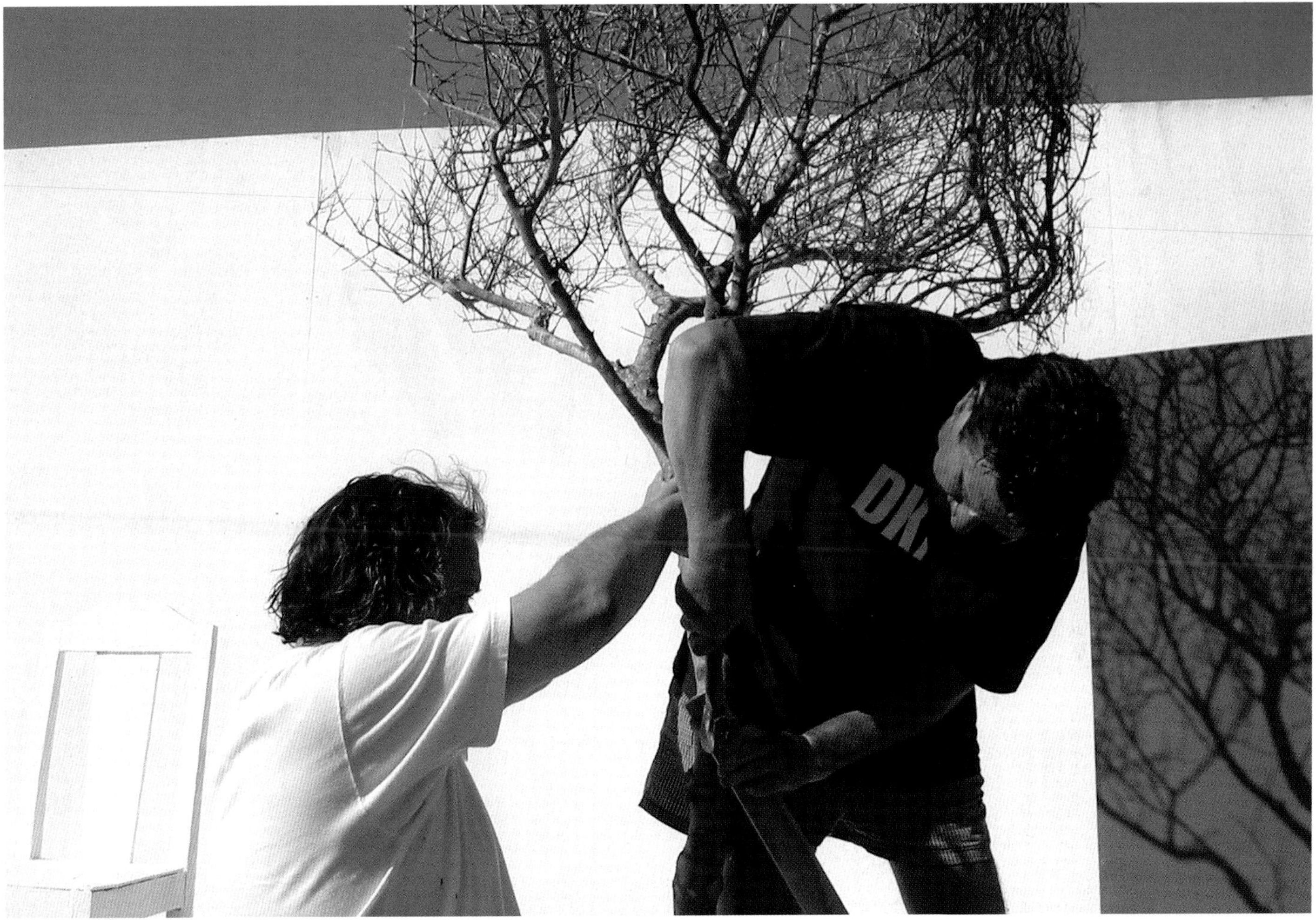

the arch of art is a place for a public view of whitehall
the mall and northumberland avenue   it is not a place for a private view
squaring the square and addressing admiralty arch   referencing the gate of the kiss
framing the endless column and the new table of silence in parliament   square
the structure of this great work of wonderment (see q.e.2, in trafalgar   square)
will be determined by the
artists   architects   scientists   engineers   philosophers
writers   composers and builders   that it will house   academic decisions about now
where   who   what and when   will not be tolerated   the artists
architects   etc   will be celebrated at all times and all creative decisions
will be upheld and implemented   art will be in the hands of the artists
and not in the minds of government officers   out of their minds   into our hands
and out of the window   the work is the arch and the arch is the work
ahaus to house great works of art -

no harvey nichols fat of skinny hang window display attitudes   no installations
no air conditioning as a tack on con   no education programme   no administration
no curation   no directors   no keepers   no security   no sponsors
no patrons   no experts   no academics   no texts   no theories
no commissions   no speciality shopping   no franchised restaurants
no parties   no private views   no logos

art is the way   not in the way of art
ref. wayside pulpit   early conceptual street works - sites specific
90% of the cost of the building   which will not be repositioned   stored
exhibited   auctioned   or deconstructed from the time to time in other buildings
stored dust   censored   removed   or   repositioned
recontextualised   and   buried   under the great museums of dust

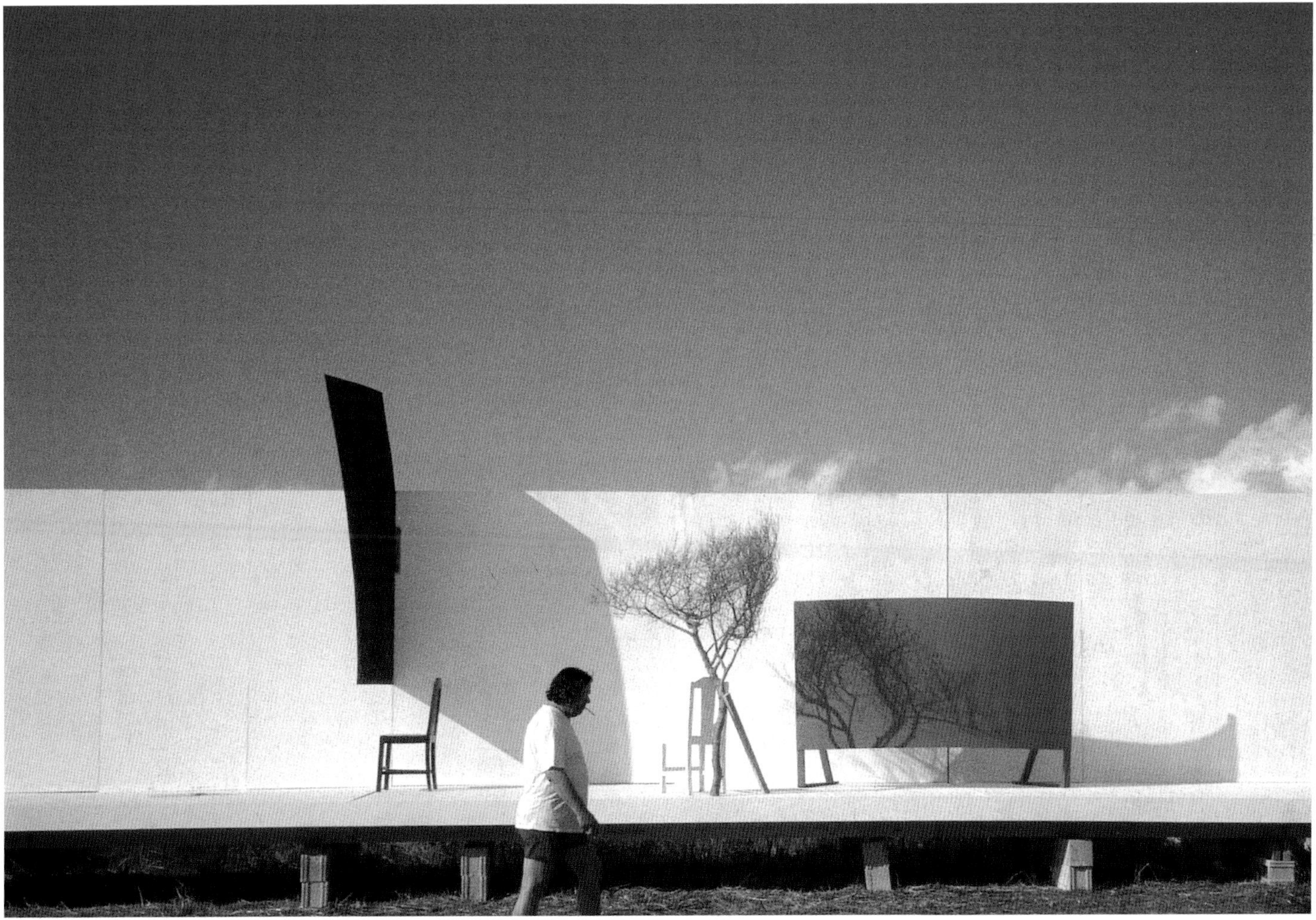

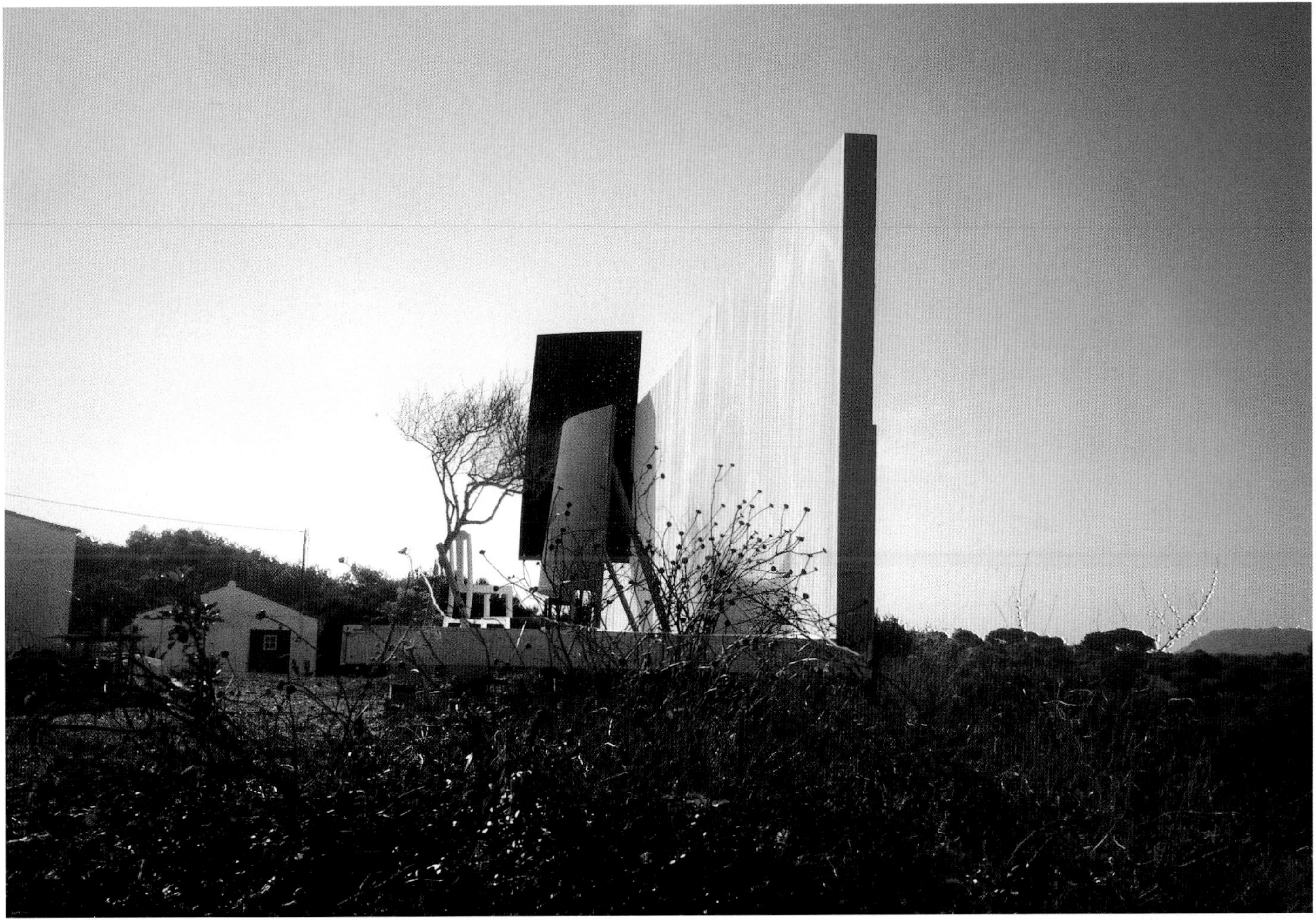

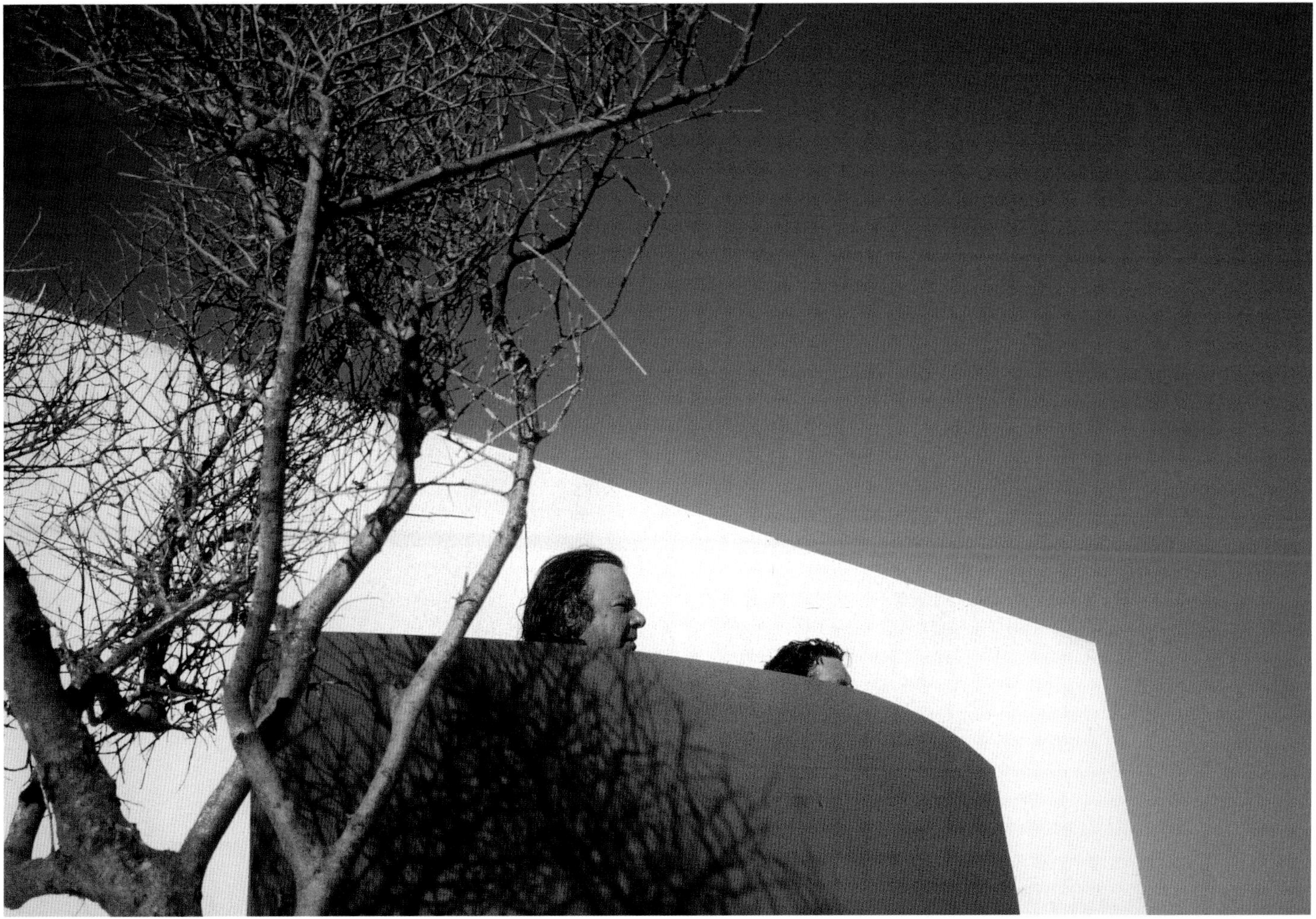

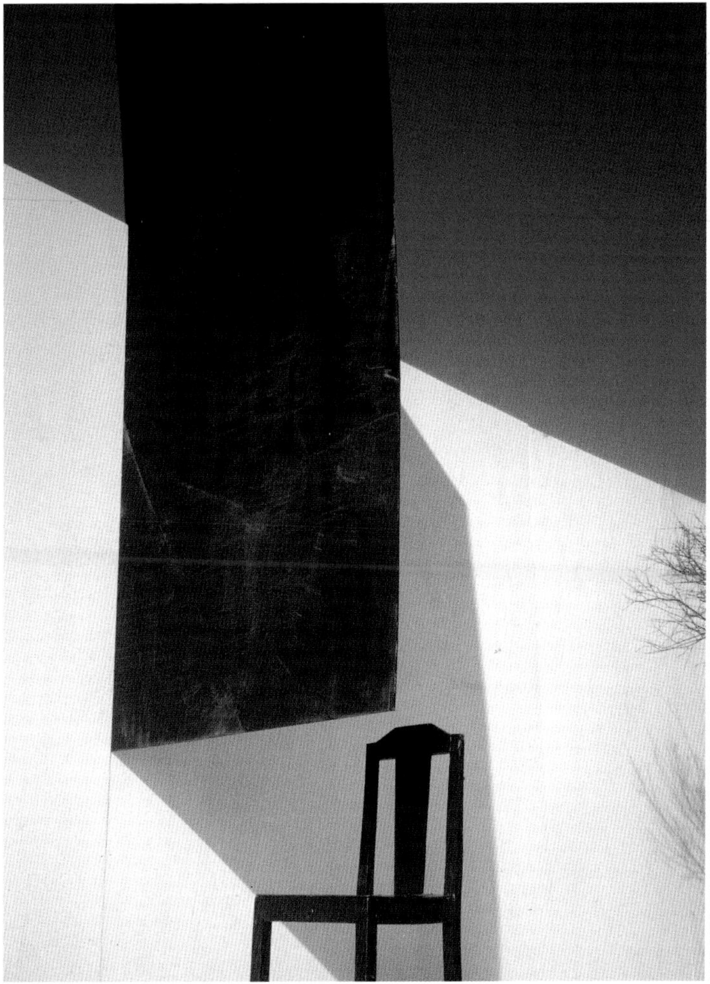

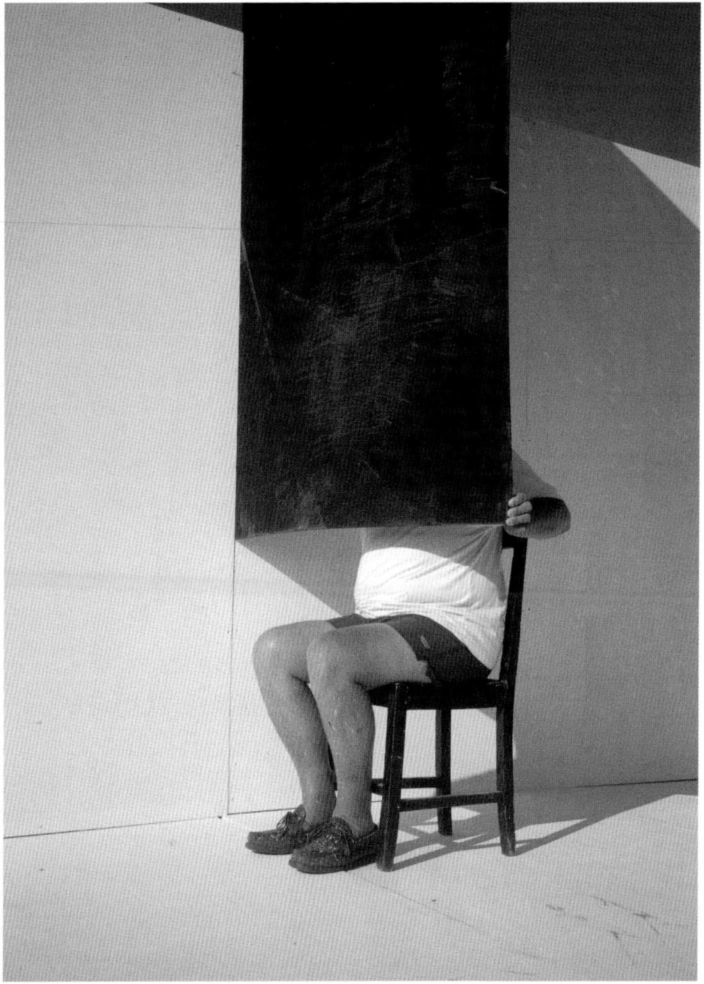

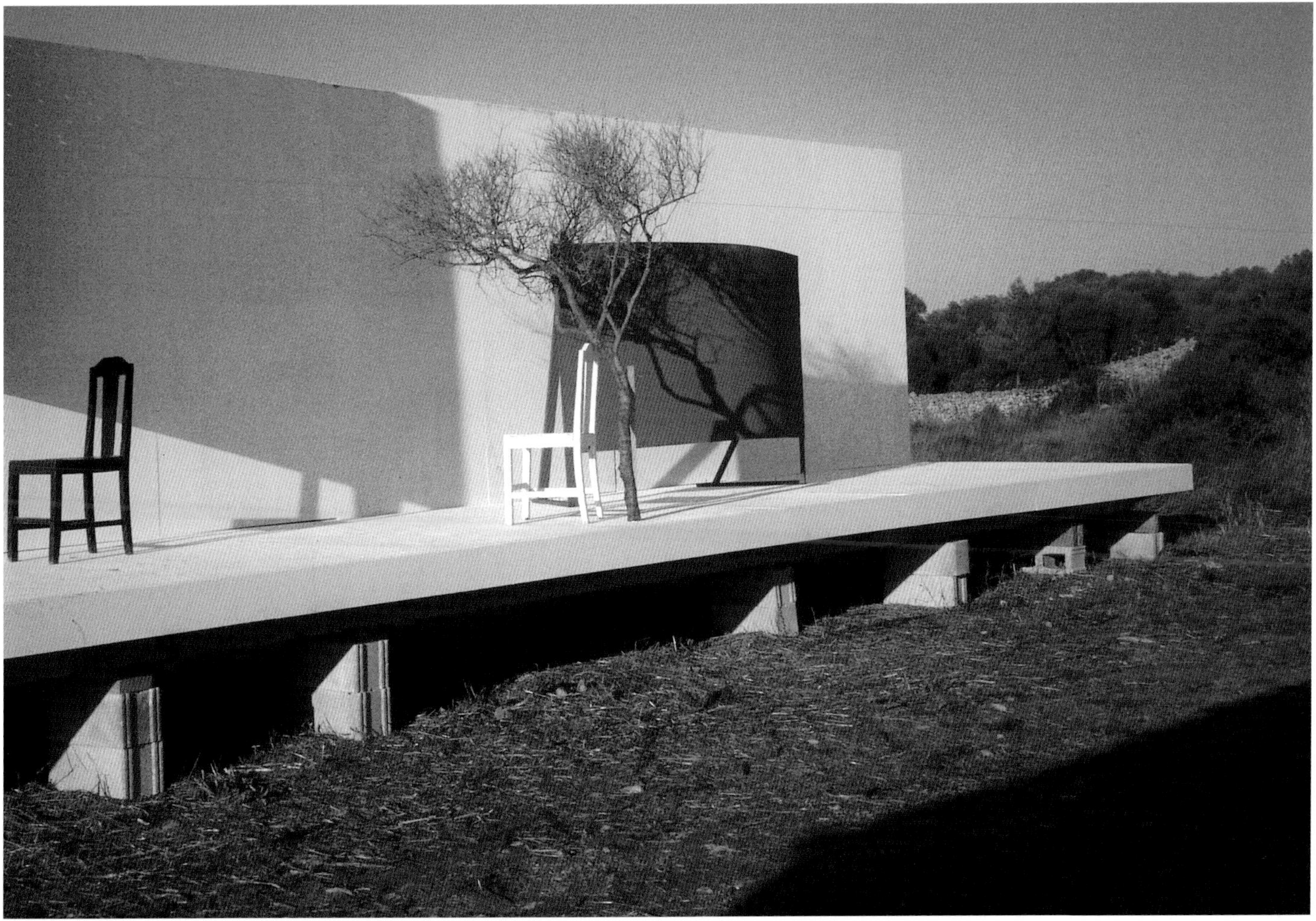

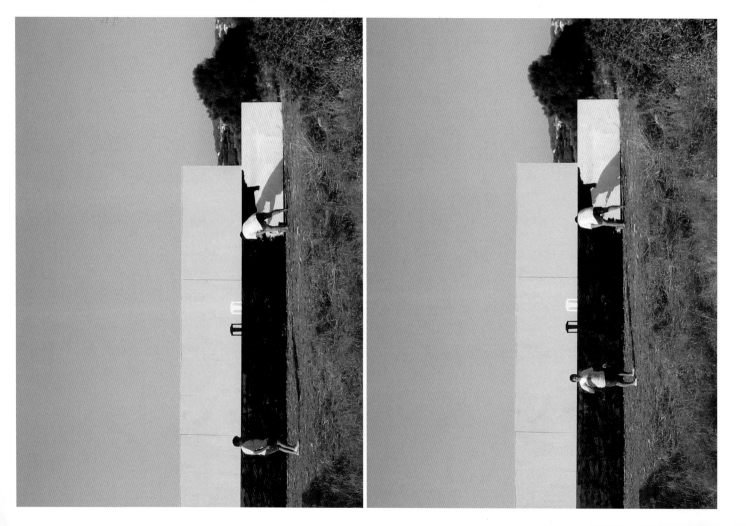

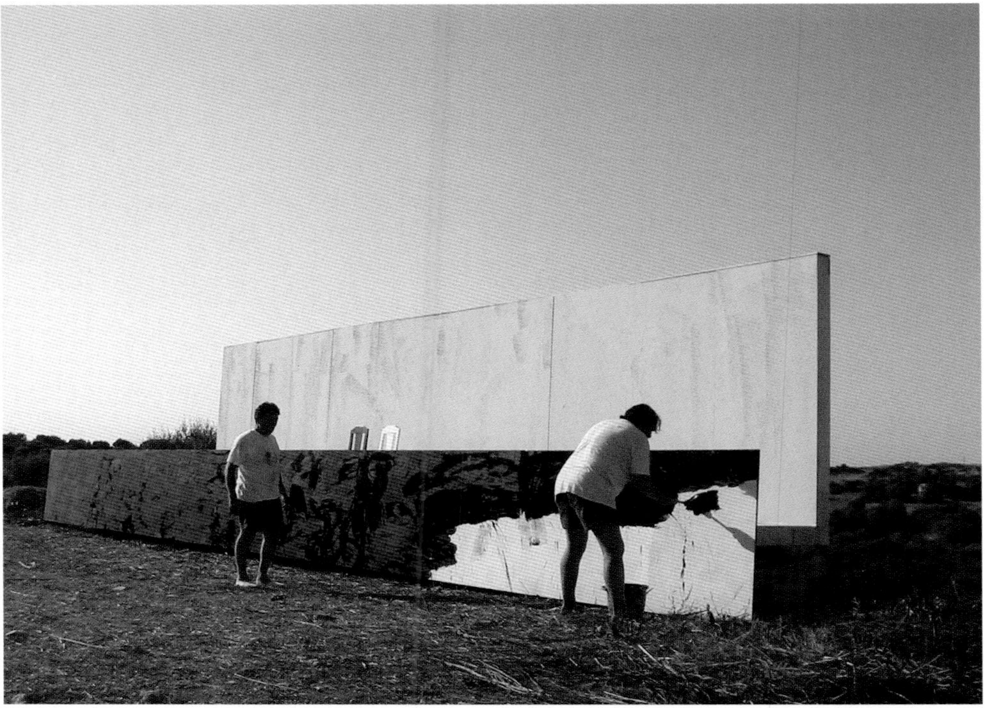

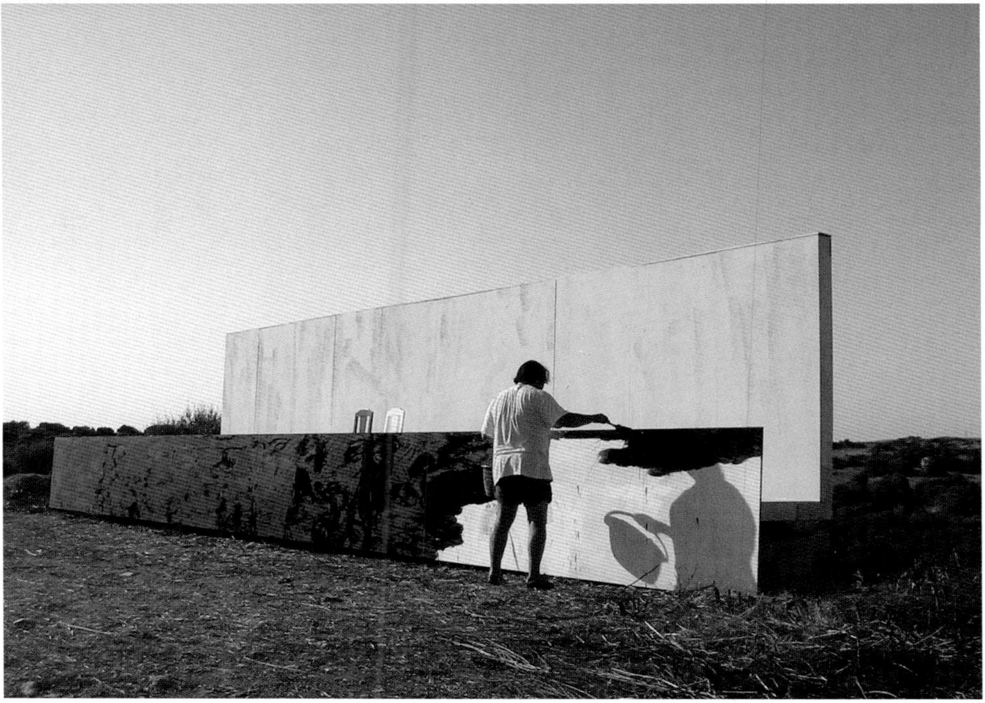

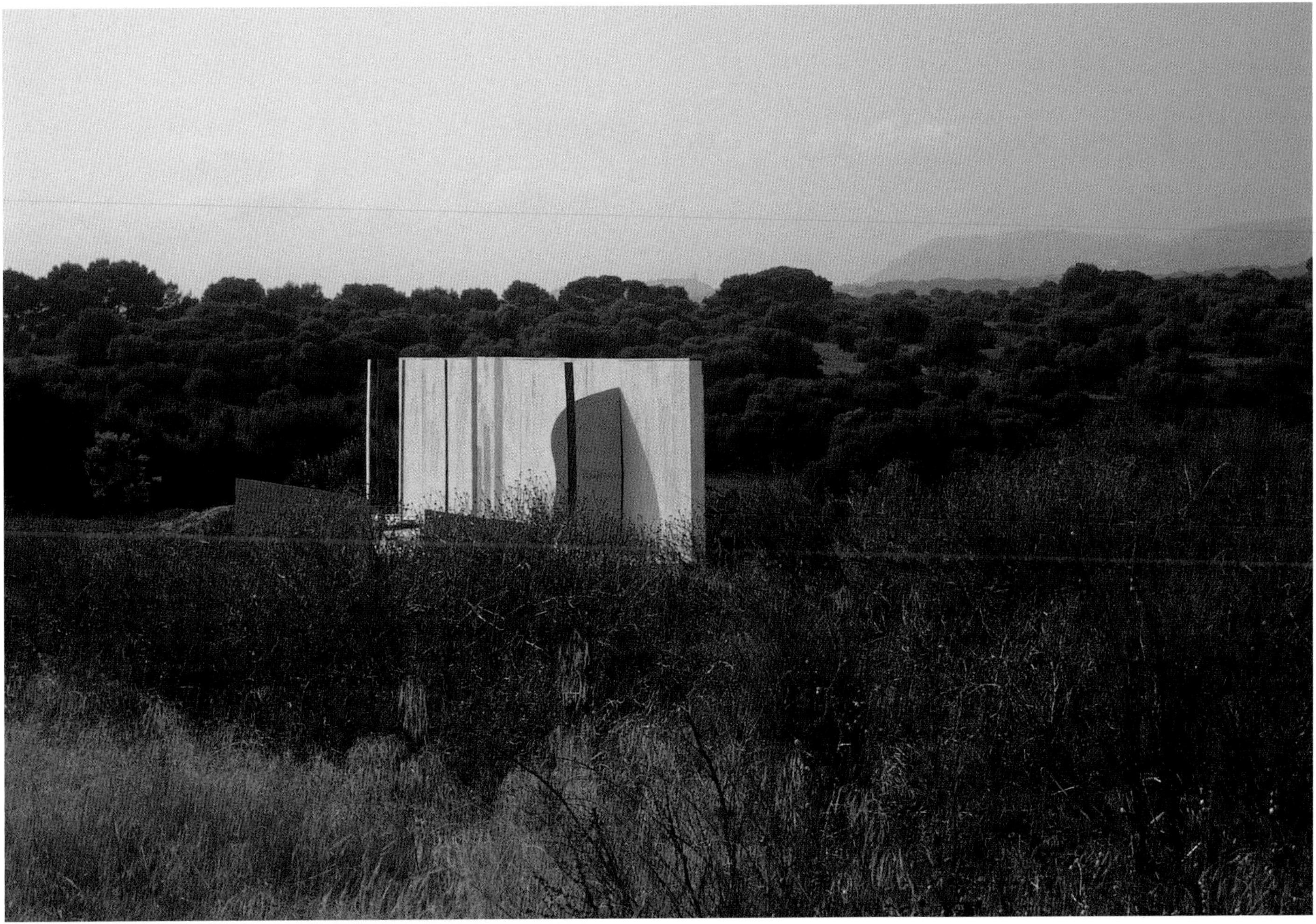

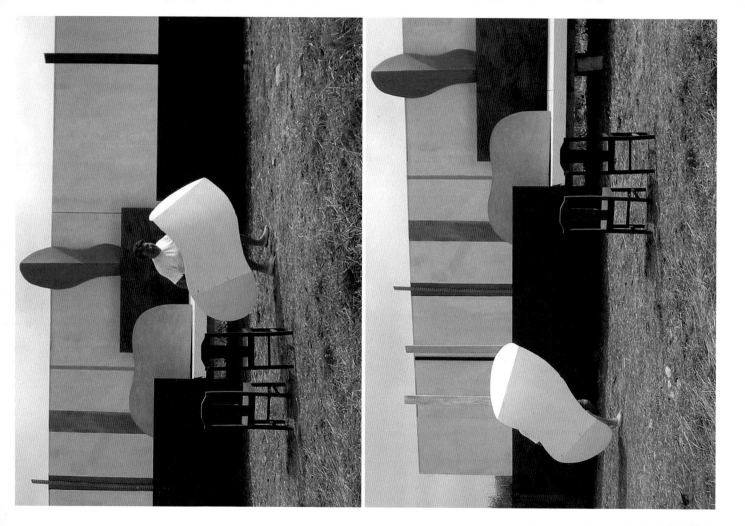

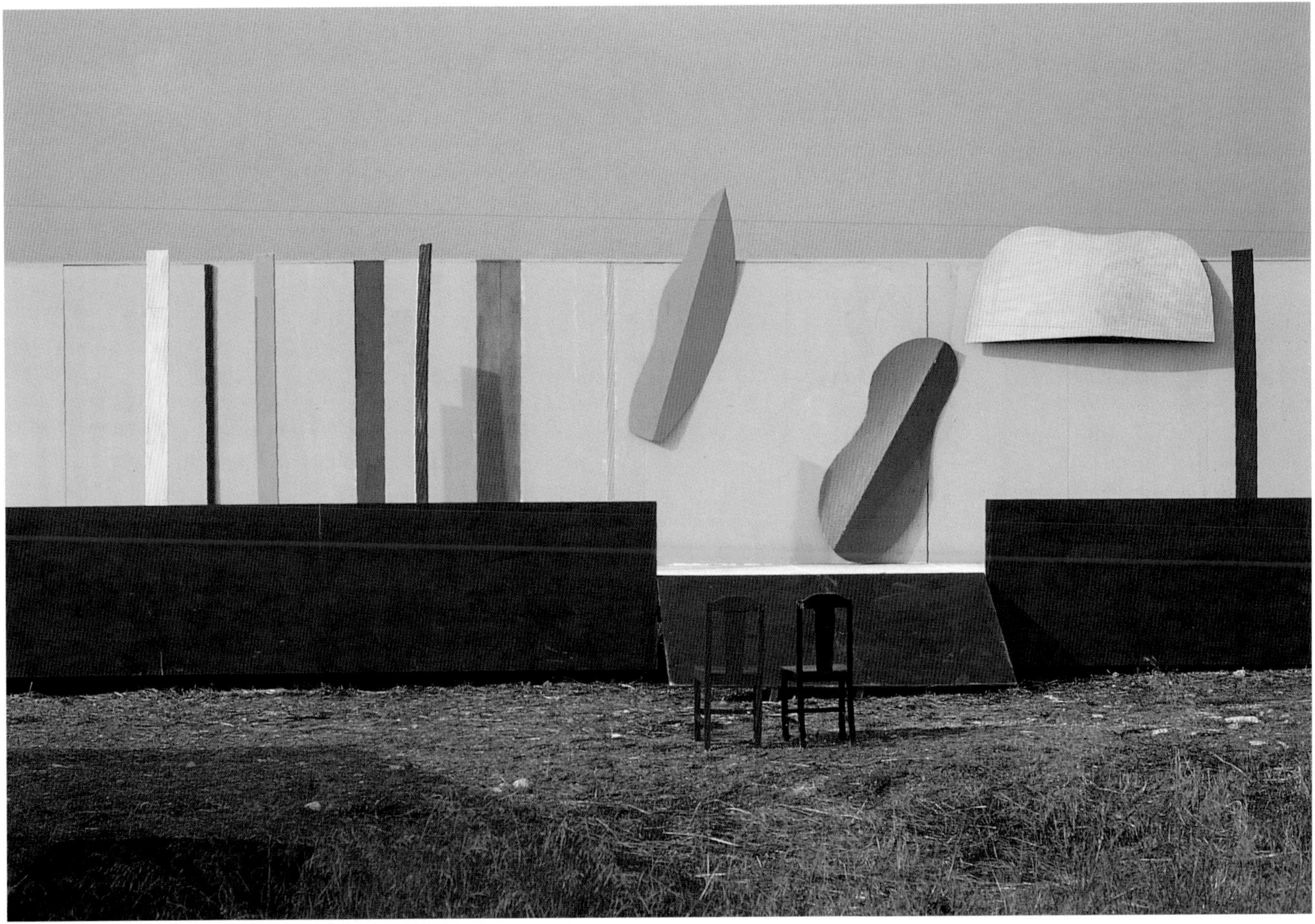

brown windsor soup and the signal of the tortoise
the   need to return to superficiality and style
the   desire for good manners or physical violence
the   ability to enter a room choosing a suitable exit
            or two how to be seen and not to be seen to be etc
            ref. lawrence weiner to see and to be seen
the   future is behind us 100 projects for the 21st century

brown windsor soup   the signal of the tortoise   outfits for life
a study of the twentieth century male earing   a world without glue   rock pose punk
modern exits   laterday doors   the dunces hat   the artists hat   the hat of the poet
a man with a hat for every occasion   a house of art   a house of hats   a house of tranquillity
negatives as positives   everything in the world is drawn   art history backwards   the car park
the art park   what is stated is not what is meant   the constant use of error
management madness   tests sites for all   the first barrel vault   a palm tree
the 8 x 4 problem   the end of entertainment   art history backwards
the square tyre and the road to no where   the building for no one   anti social housing schemes
in the theme world scheme world   the theatre of the normal   grey flannel cinema
the end of art the end for art   after art discussion   tv programmes for the 21st century
the curator crisis   ref. crease crisis   any clues there for the Hercule Poirot of the critical theoretical
I've found a clue   the cross word art work problem   piece problem   investigations into testing trying
and destroying   achieving the ability to forget and not to bother to document anything at all
the absence of documentation   the new school of thoughtlessness   meeting connecting
and disconnecting   the story of pose   life before masking tape   a world with no glue
the end of art   the art school project   no projects   a short history of non verbal communication
a study of patterns of behaviour   a series of rooms for very different activities   the architecture
determines the activities   sexual sport   book of ideas contradicting normal academic thought
a book of seasons   a book for all seasons   a manifesto   a parliament
a village hall   a station   a circle of art
inner and outer paths of knowledge   no themes   no topics   no projects
no ideas   places for ideas to develop   drawings and texts

discuss the idea of buildings being conceived of and constructed for no one

buildings for no one   places for no one
the necessity to design and consider the people who will inhabit the buildings for no one
connections misinterpreted misread misinformed
ideas thoughts facts and lies
the thoughts behind the thoughts
place process positions point prophesy
predict produce pronounce pretend parody   a kilometre theatre
best seat best view etc   determine new works for stage street promenade
a street car named desire   over 1 kilometre   waiting for more than half an hour for Godot
a celebration of a traffic jam with real cars   a traffic jam theme park   parody park
a car park   on grass   plus trees etc   a theme world out there
facade park   a park for nothing   a celebration of not being allowed to do anything in a park
no walking on the grass   no cycling   shagging   running   skateboarding
no cars or hula hoops   jogging   a building in the park to celebrate absolutely nothing
a building for the rehearsal and practising of redundant gestures   a building of tranquillity
a palace of performance   a restaurant of doors   an arrival   a study
various modern exits   a plan for london the interconnecting city
the use of fairground technology for white knuckle rides throughout the city to airports   stations etc
learning grounds
schools of thought
the dunces hat
a house of hats
1 000 000 000 000 000 000 hats

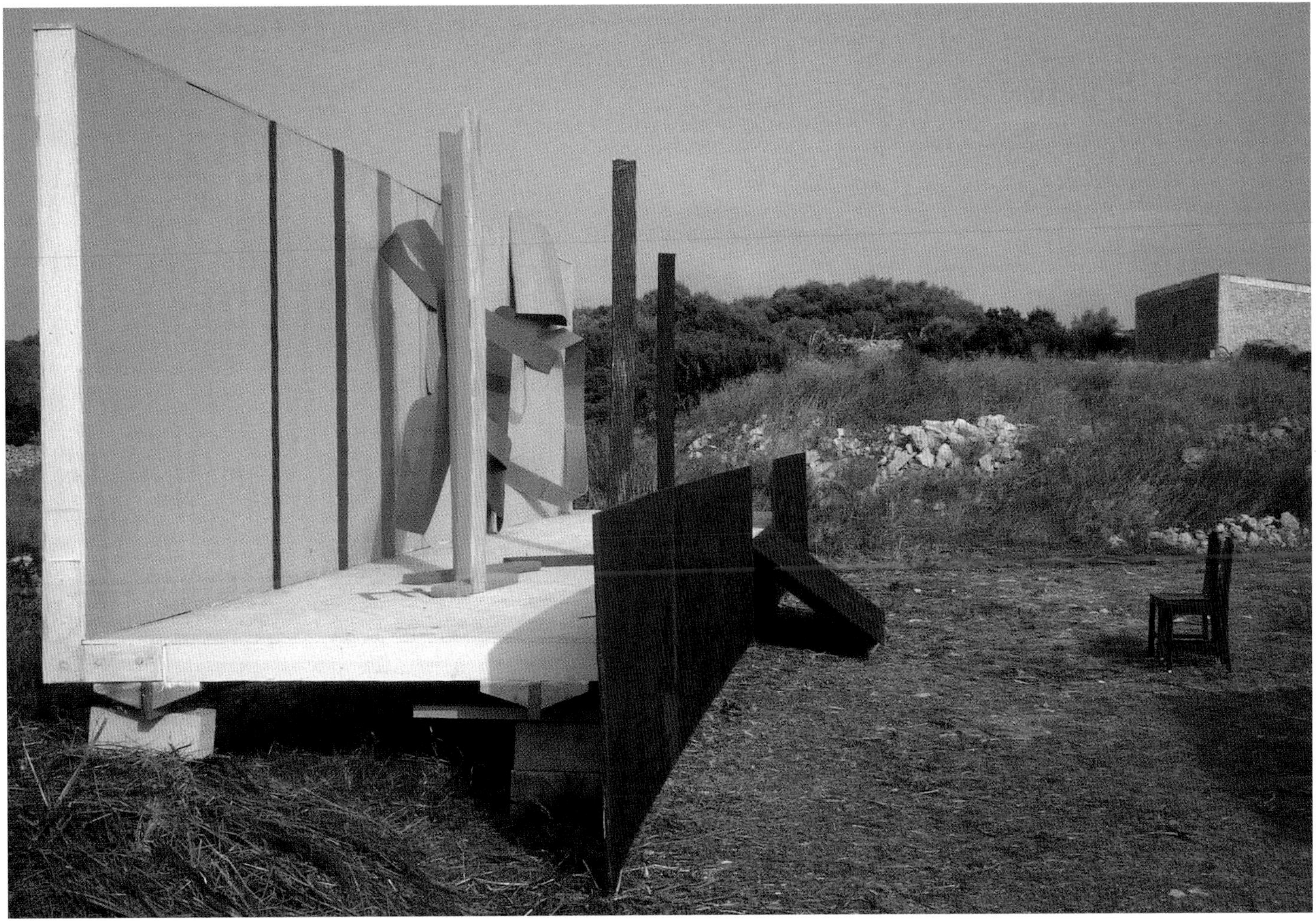

a painting
for protuberance places in the sexless society

the   drome
sin   drome
the   sexarium   muti sex for the under   stimulated
                                                                   stimulated strollers

and device dens obsession centres post avant and modern mock tudor free - form gesture areas
community   gesture
fine   gesture   etc

situated deep in graph park
centre of obsessive measurement
weight
speed
height
time
length
measured
numbered
numerated
nudist
nudge zone
above the sky invisible screened by thermal thermo static sealing
ceiling ransparent roof sun block factor canopy variable determined sun strength
morning awning sunset blind

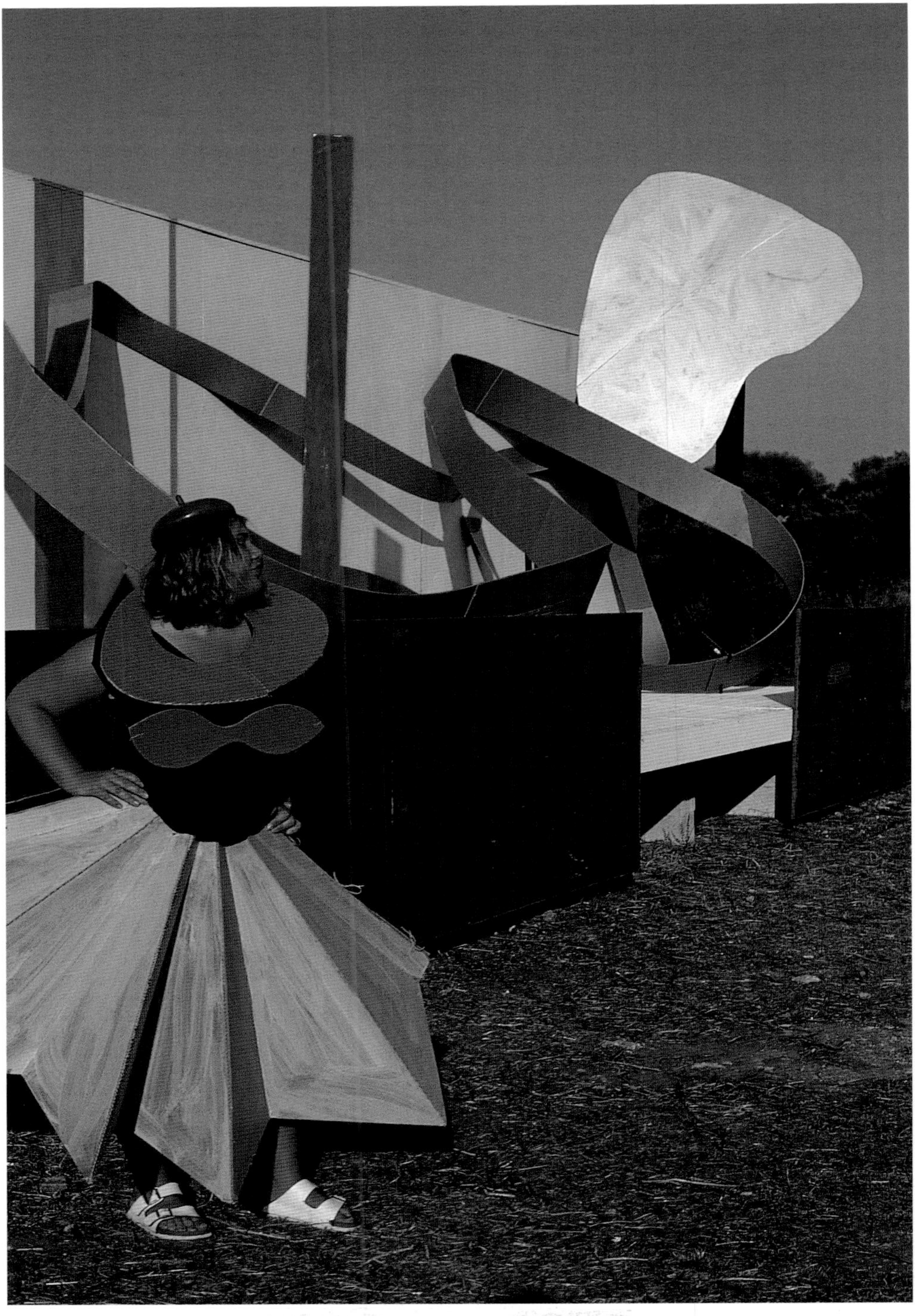

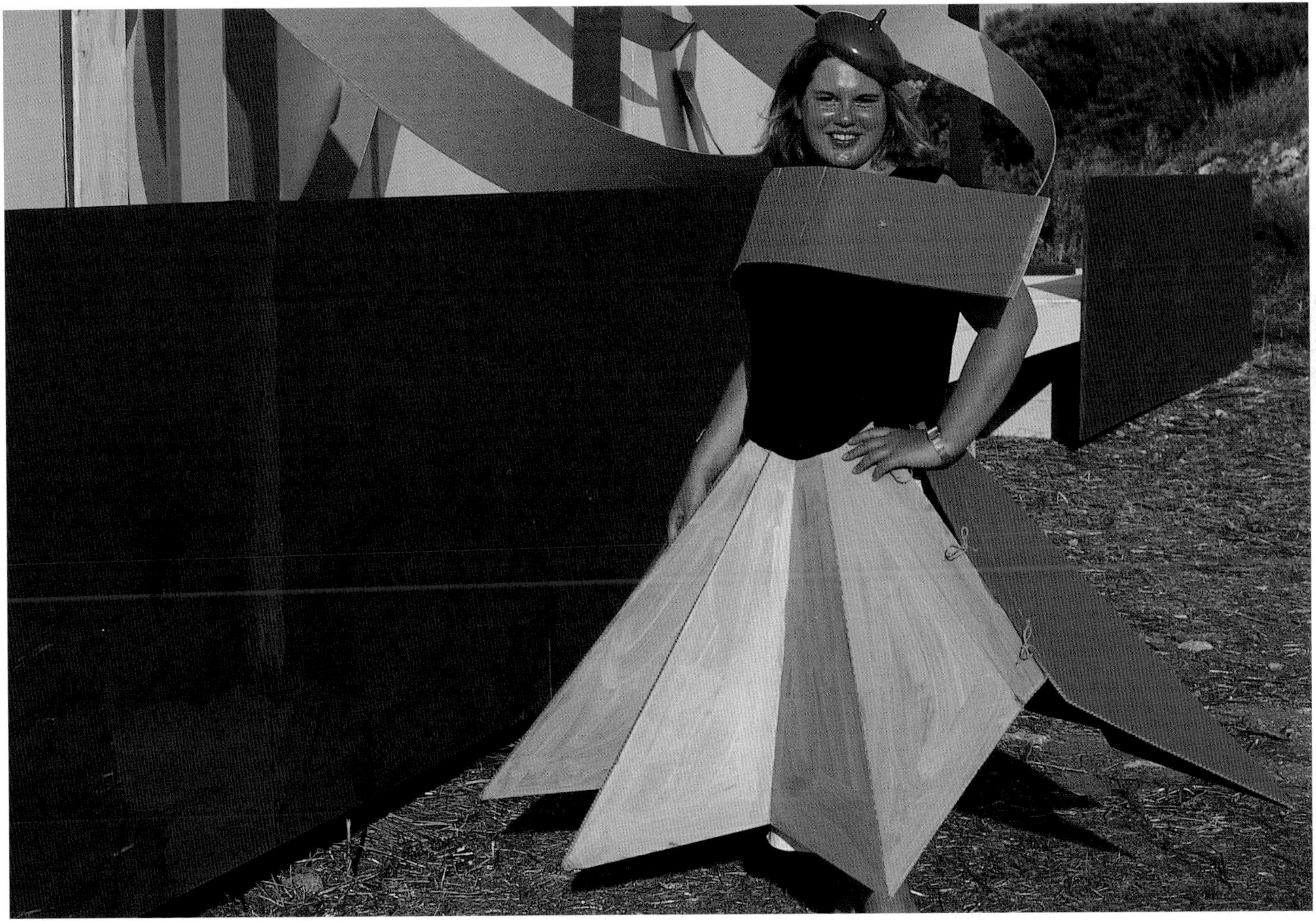

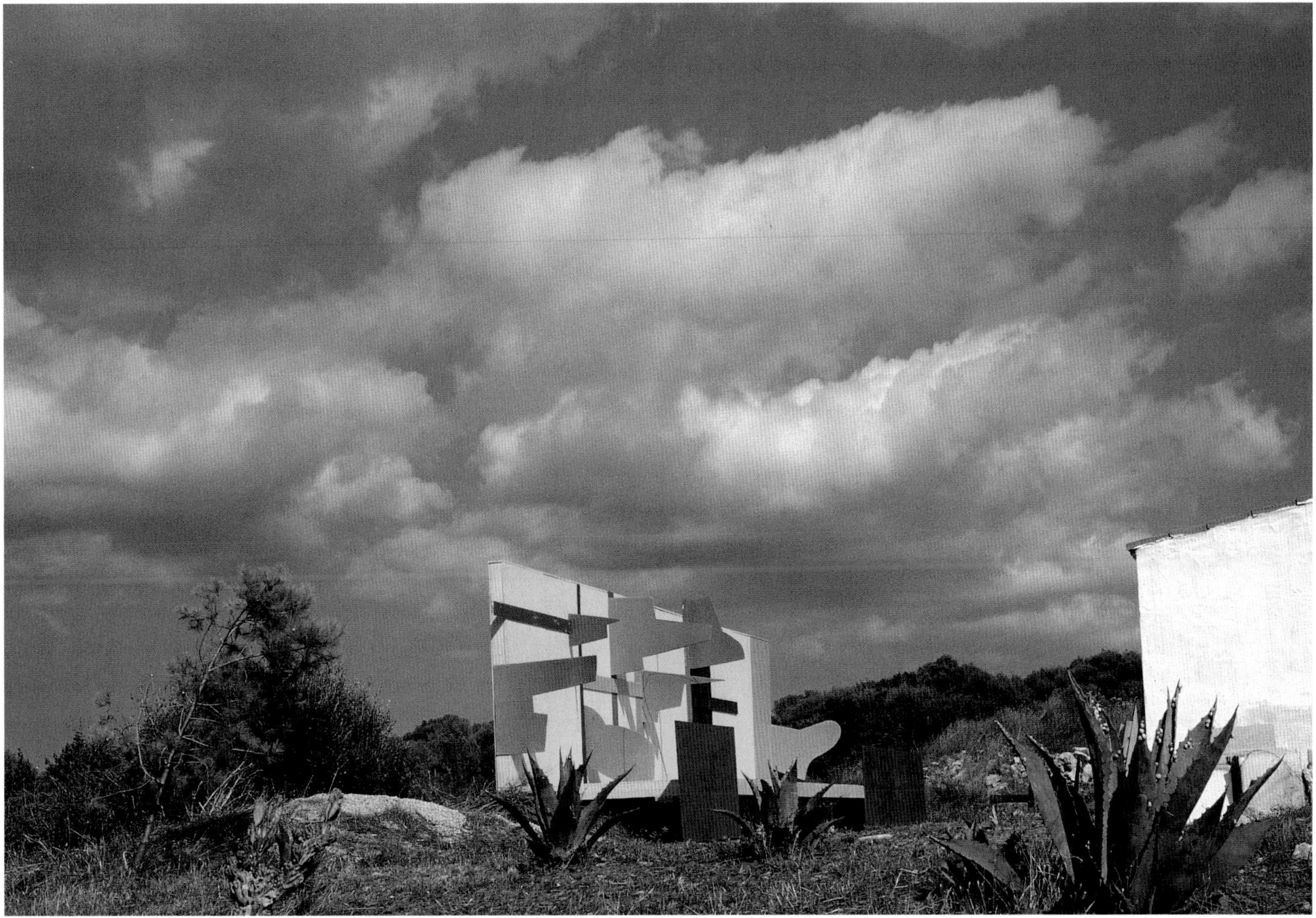

beyond the fitted kitchen cum picture window ensemble based loosely covered
ref. misinterpreted bonnard /
monet moment
and the sensational belgian butchers chopping block conversion into a skylight fixture
we address the microwave digi diner /
cool deep freeze type LA lounging pad in line with three balanced flues
on patio door onto sundeck sundial suburban submerged in spurge situations
is what makes today's master bedrooms with revived ensuite bathrooms
in avocado overlooking llama skin lined conversation pits retro
ref. p.v.c. lolla - bouts so unappealing particularly in
converted knocked through victorian propped up planted and lit habitually brick
i've got the wrong end of the stick shit houses

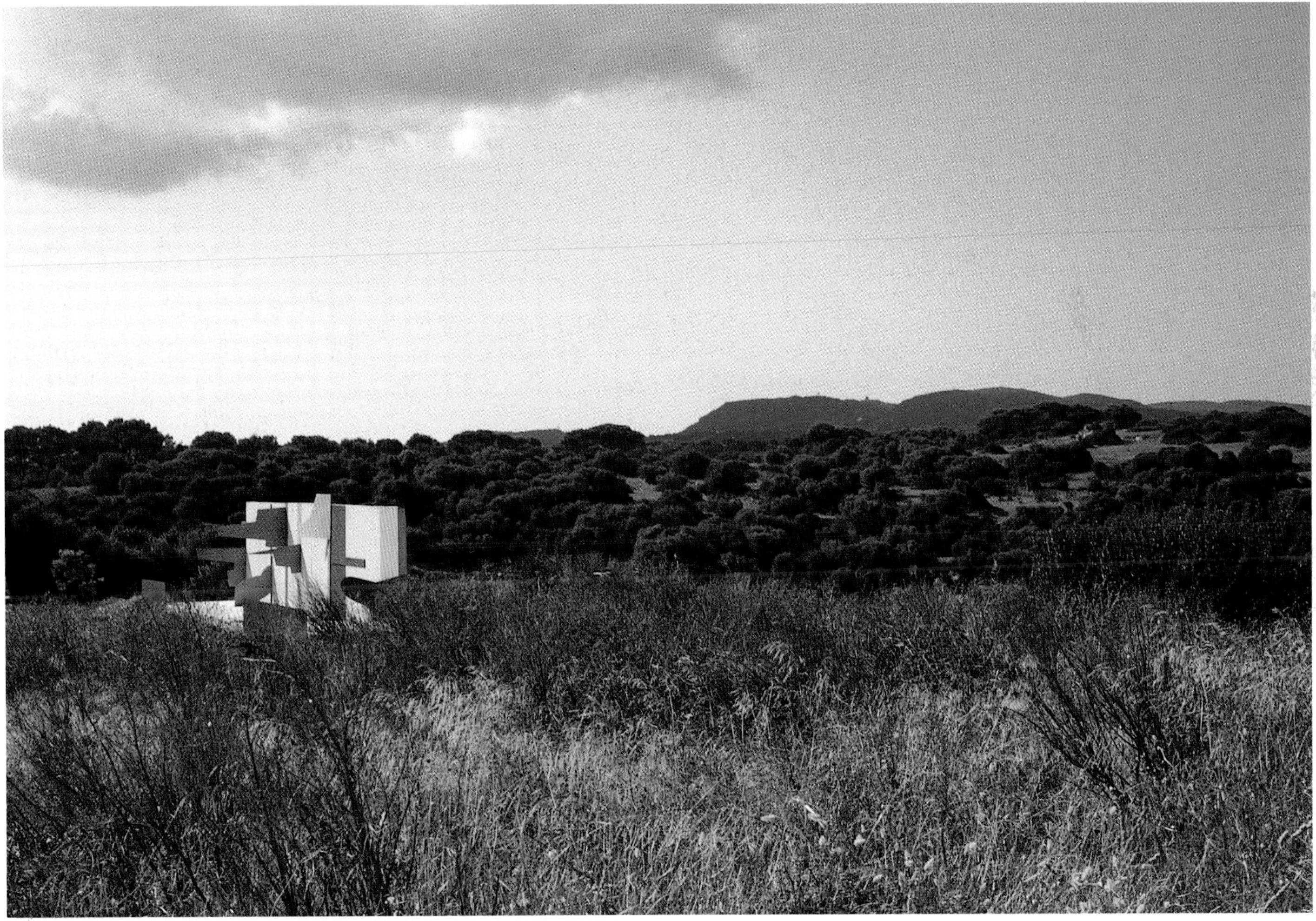

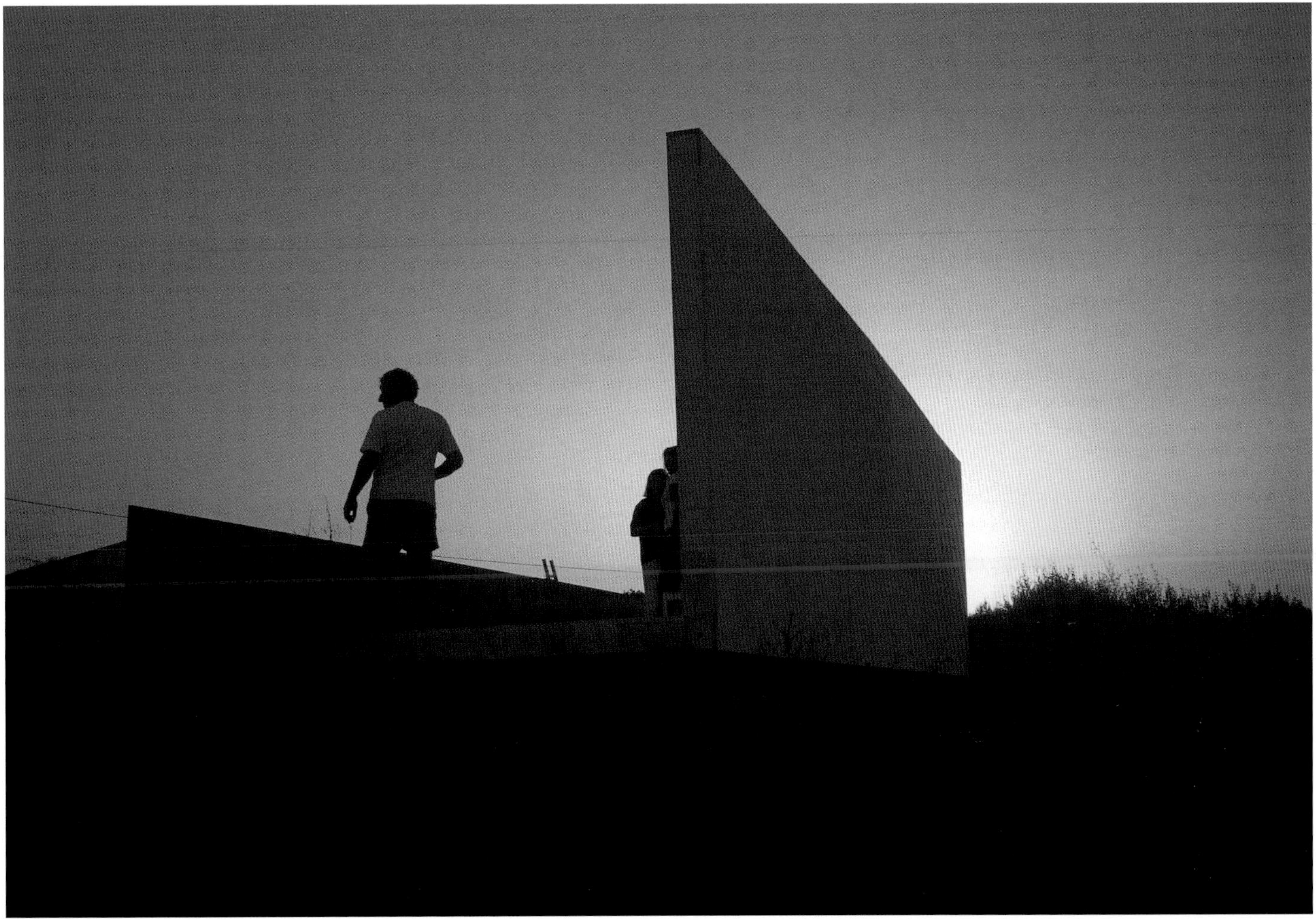

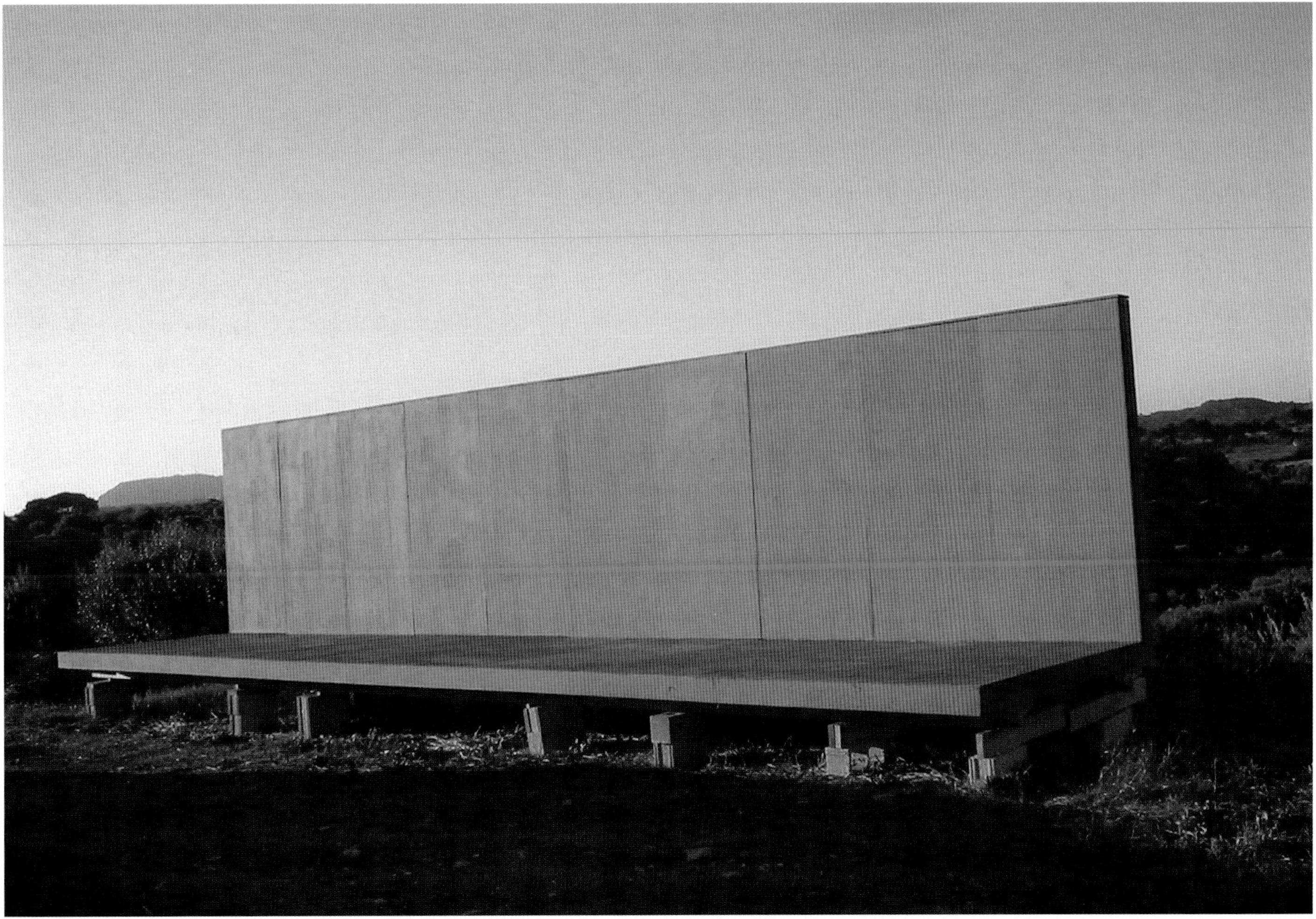

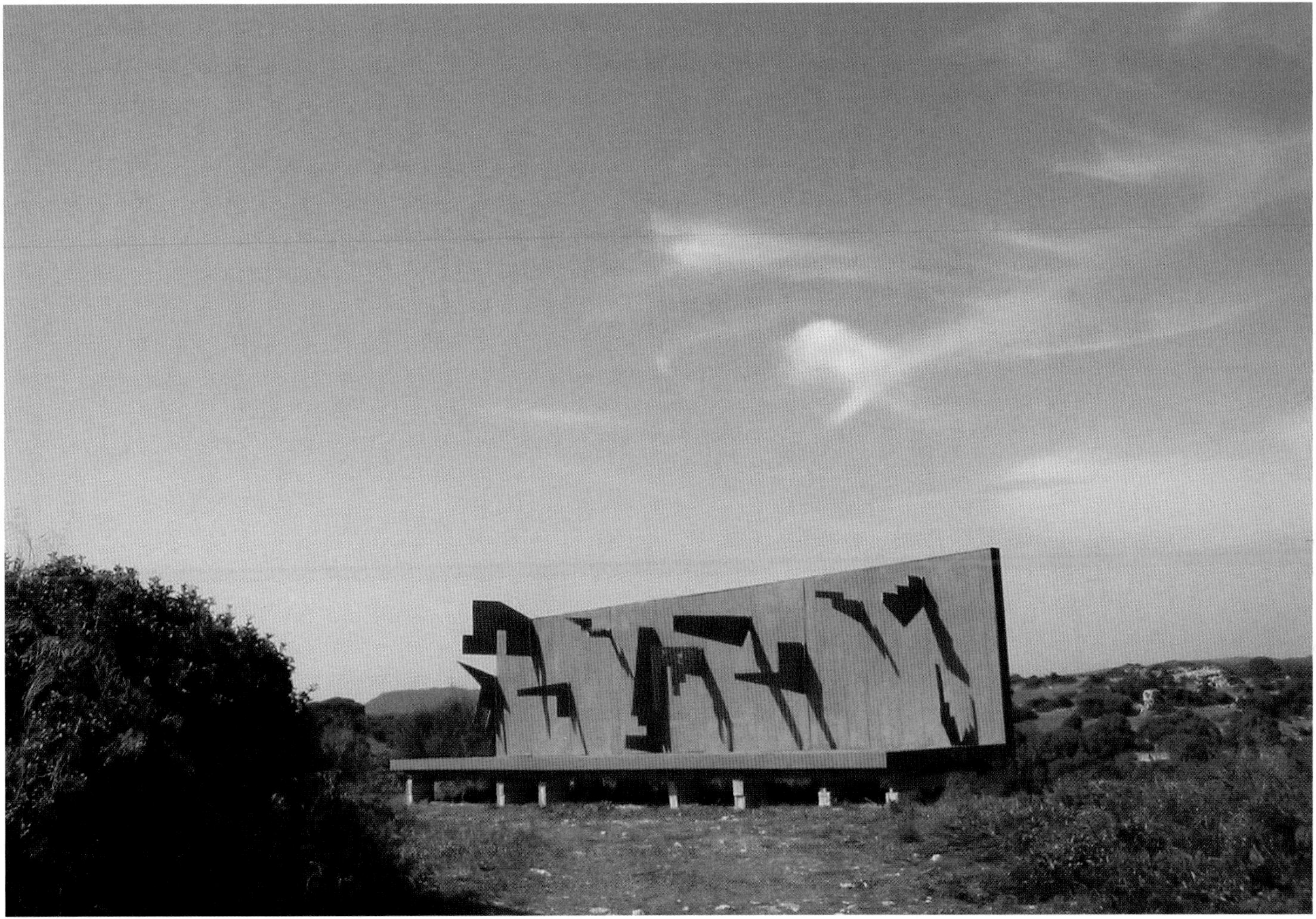

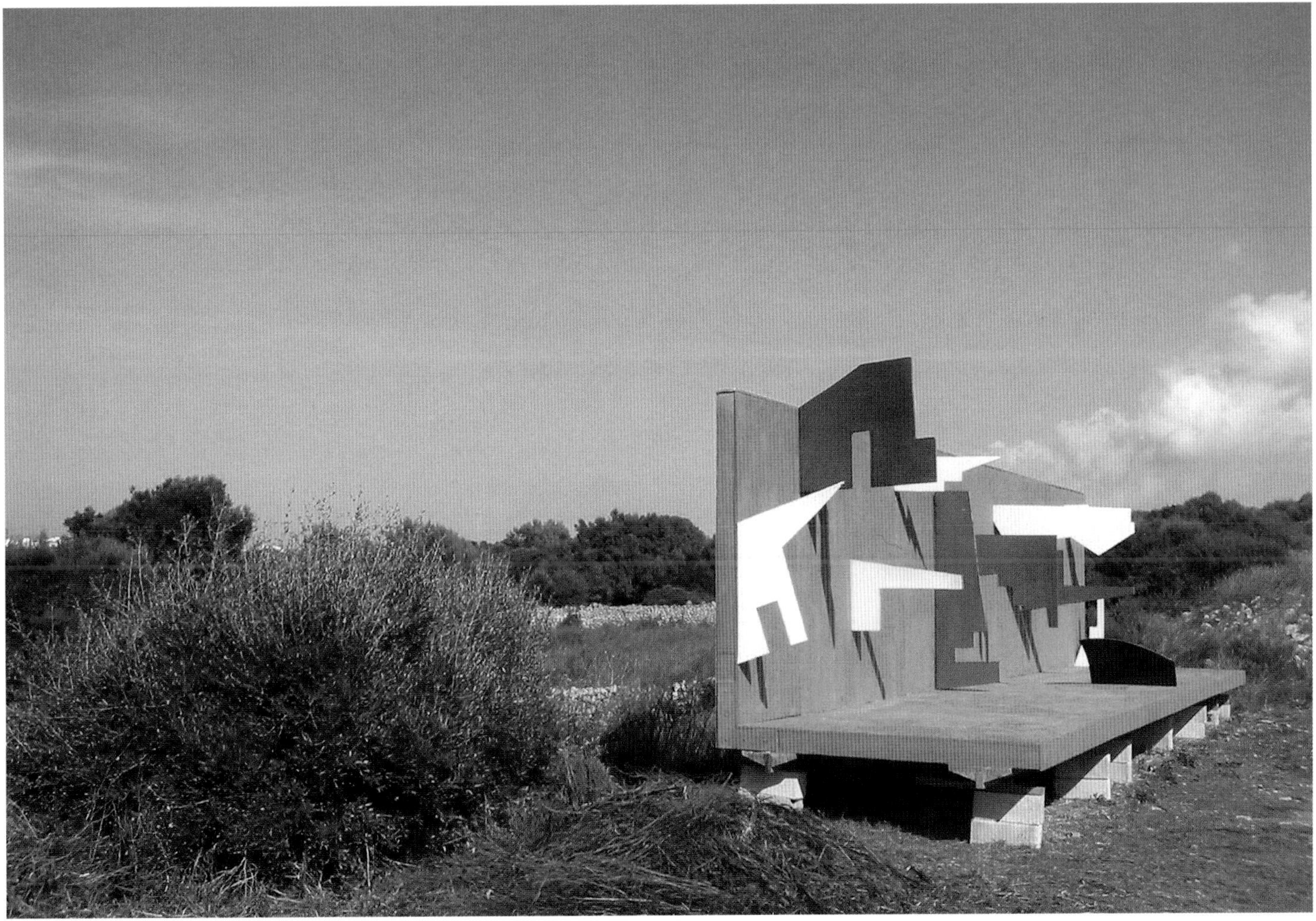

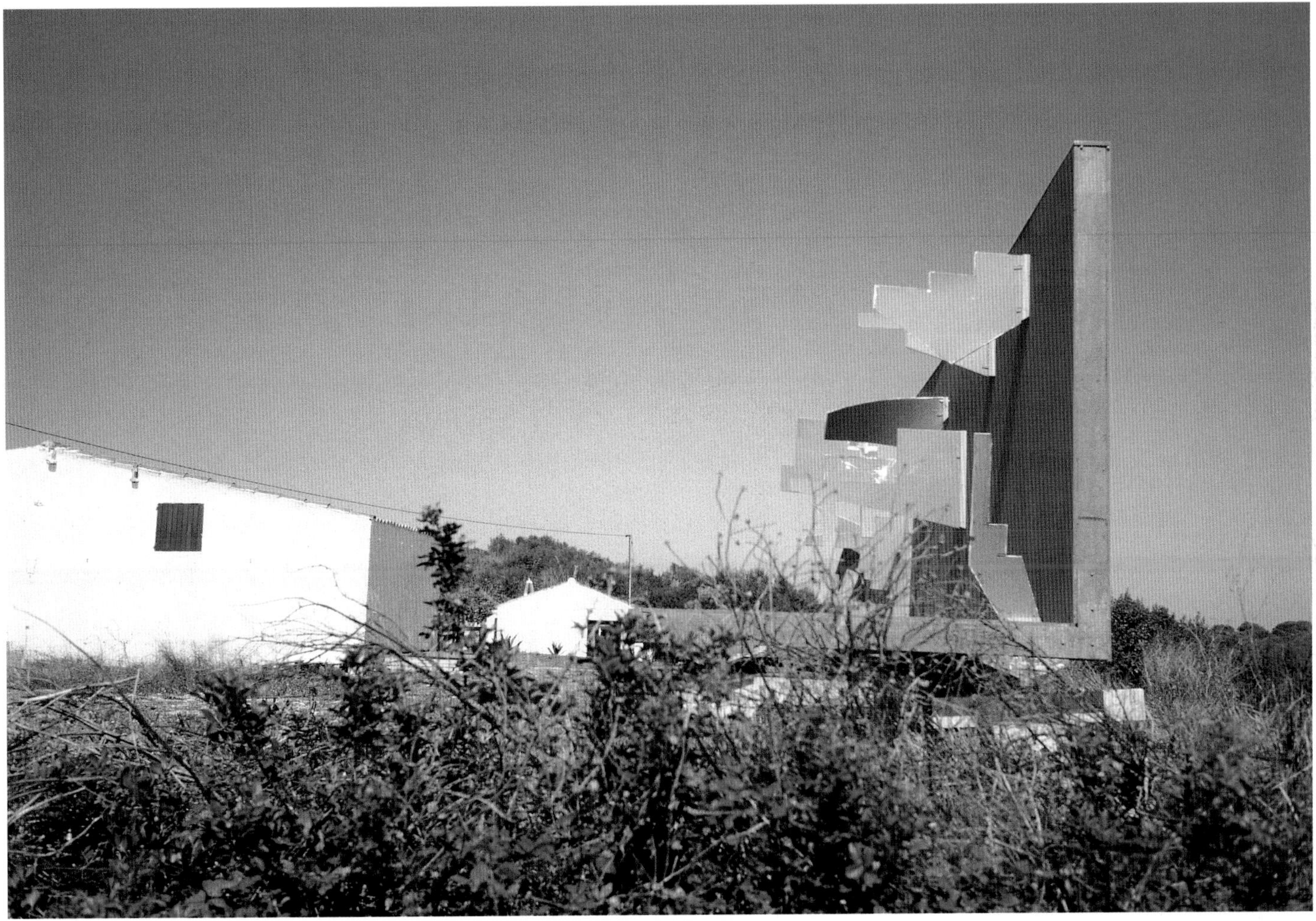

best	seat	theatre
kilometre		theatre
front	row	
best	view	

action at a distance

large moving hat obstruction plus designer shadow and corinthian column device
amplified crisp crackle crunch and malteser munch effect

free   fruit

| macbeth over a 'mile' - a street - car named desire | - | on broadway |
| modified movement and communication problems | - | can you hear me mother? |

he's beside you
750 metres

backstage   left

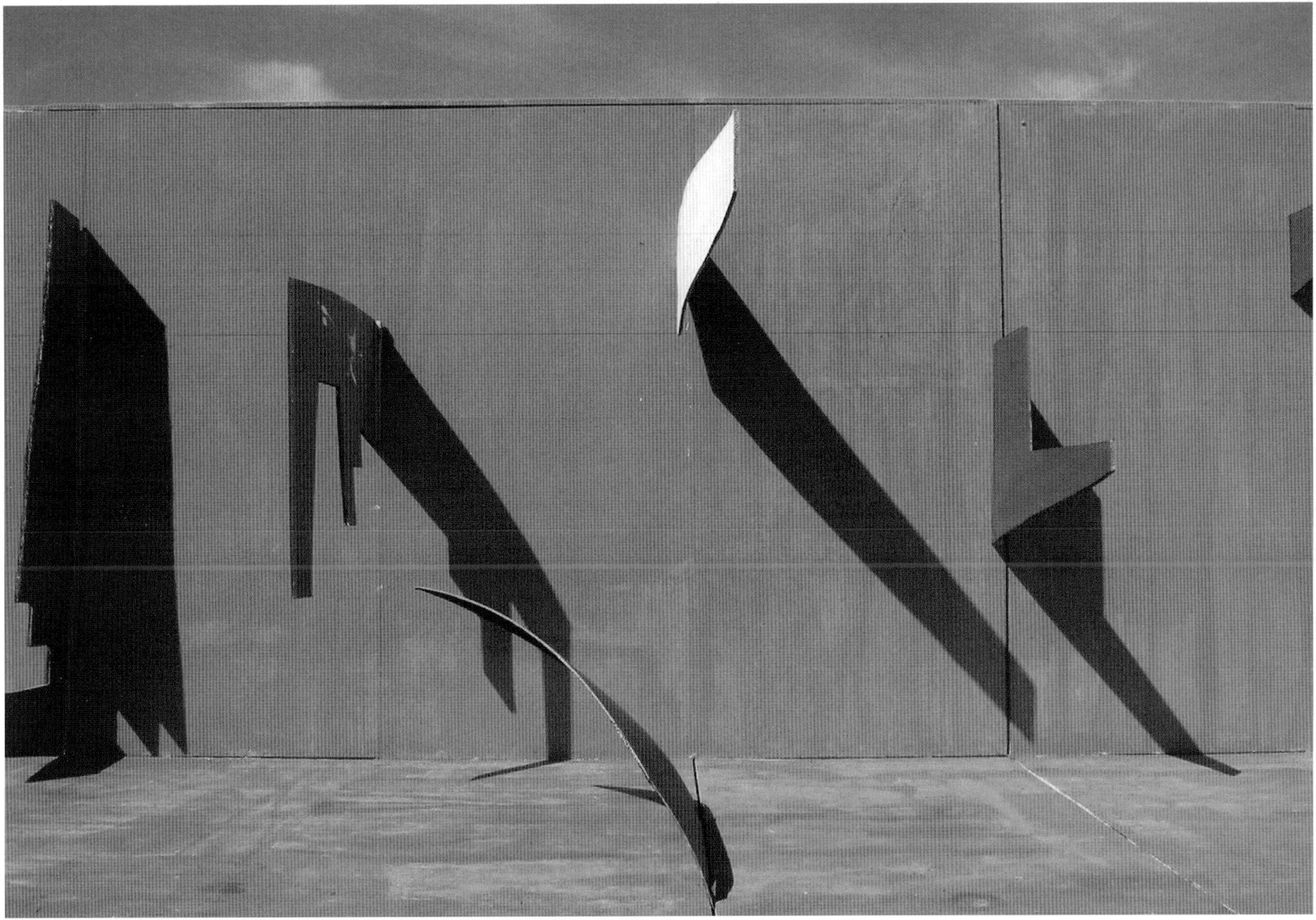

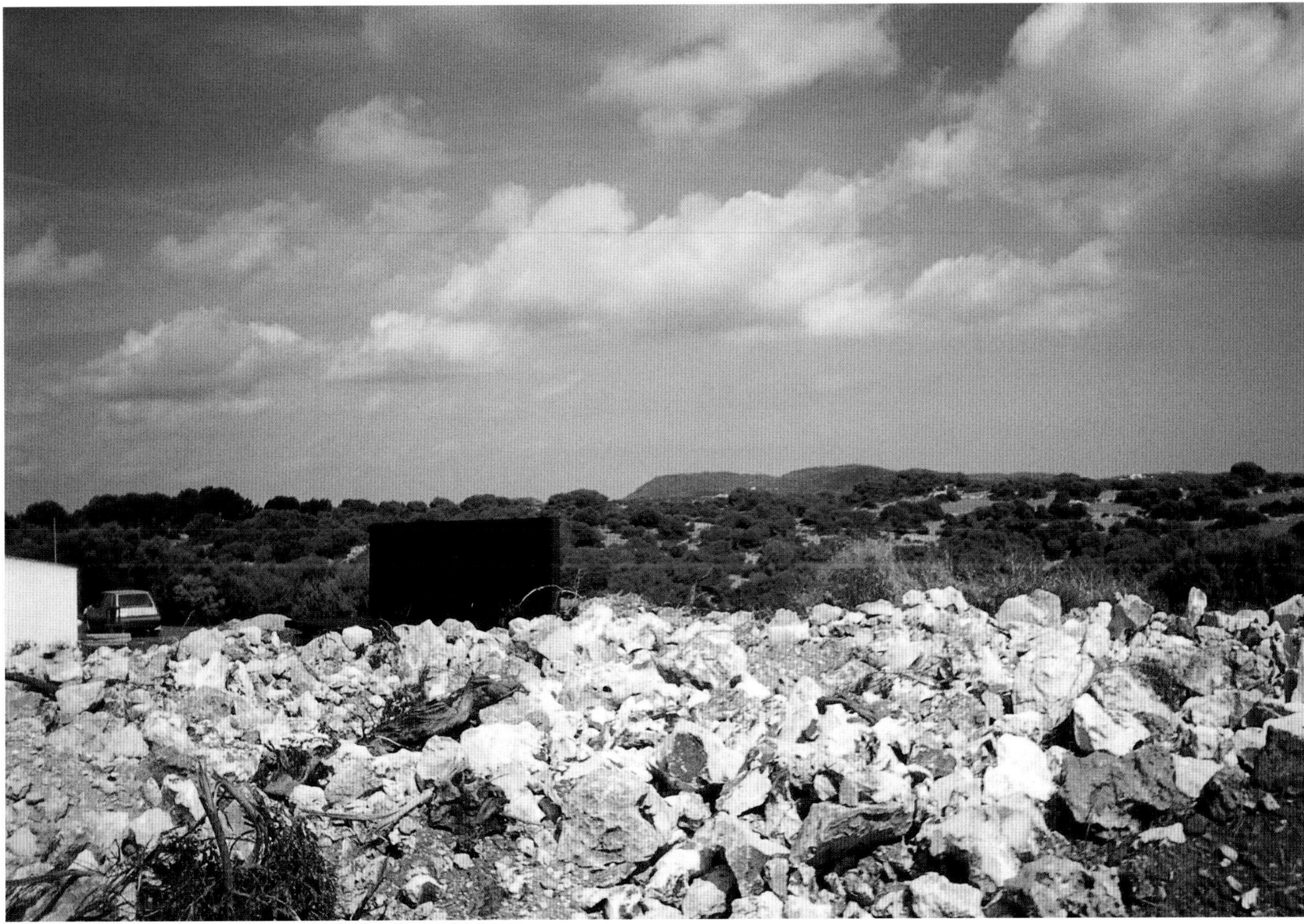

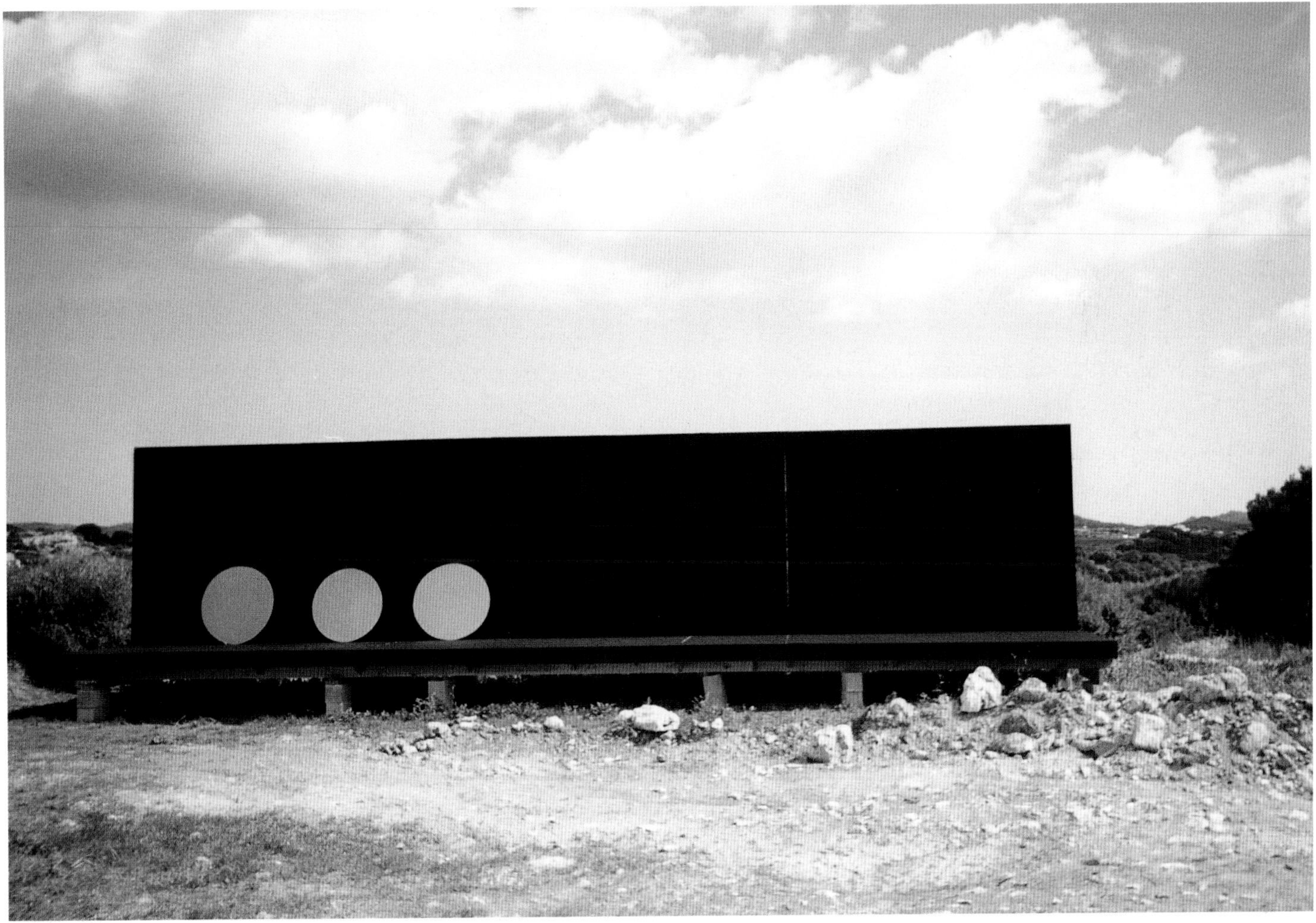

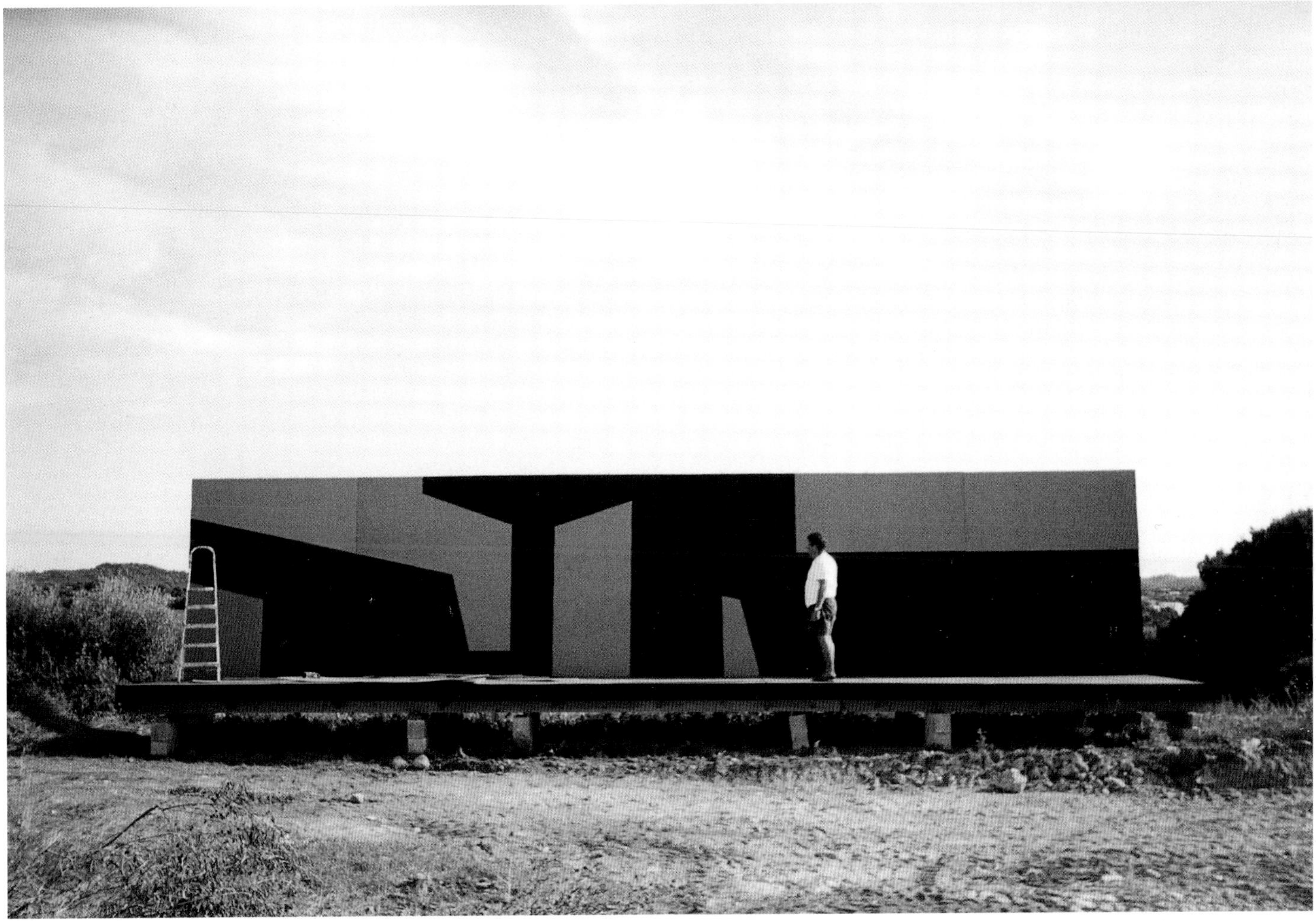

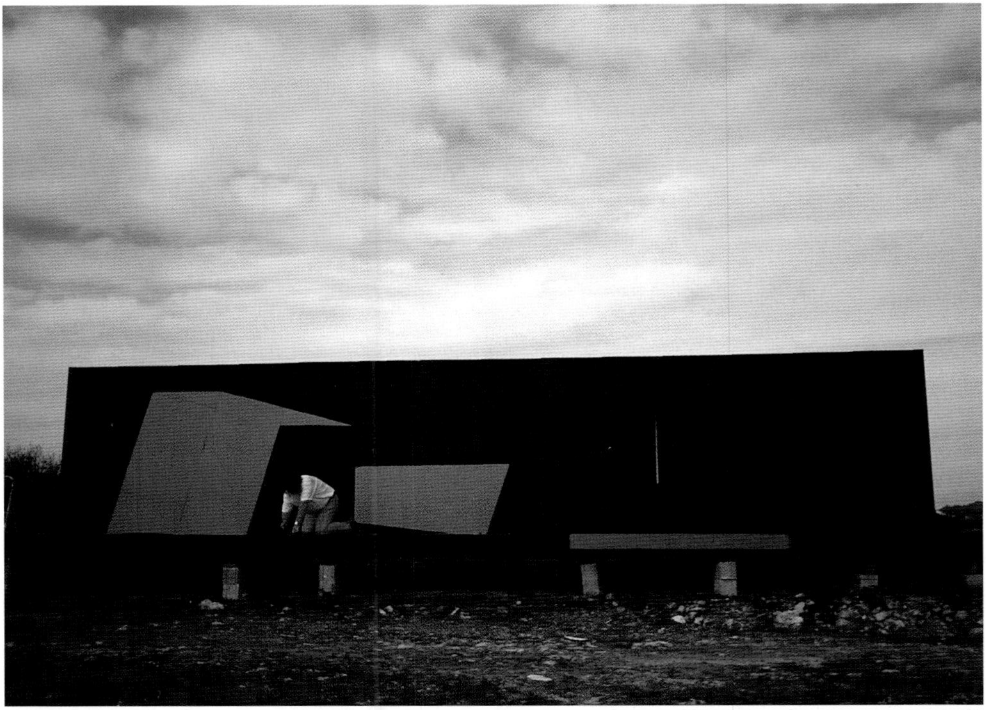

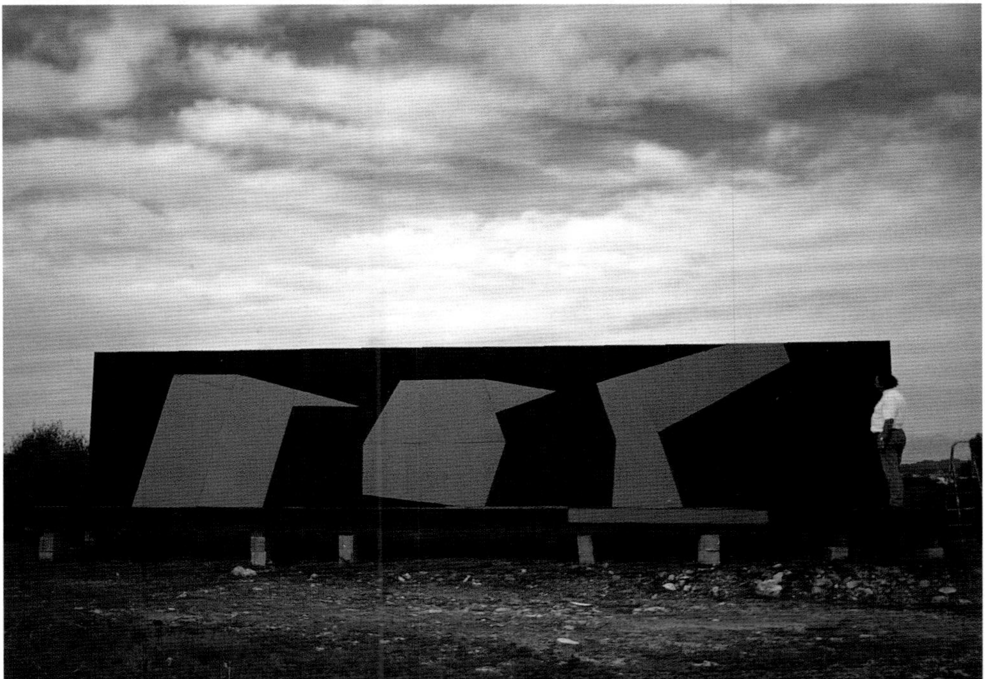

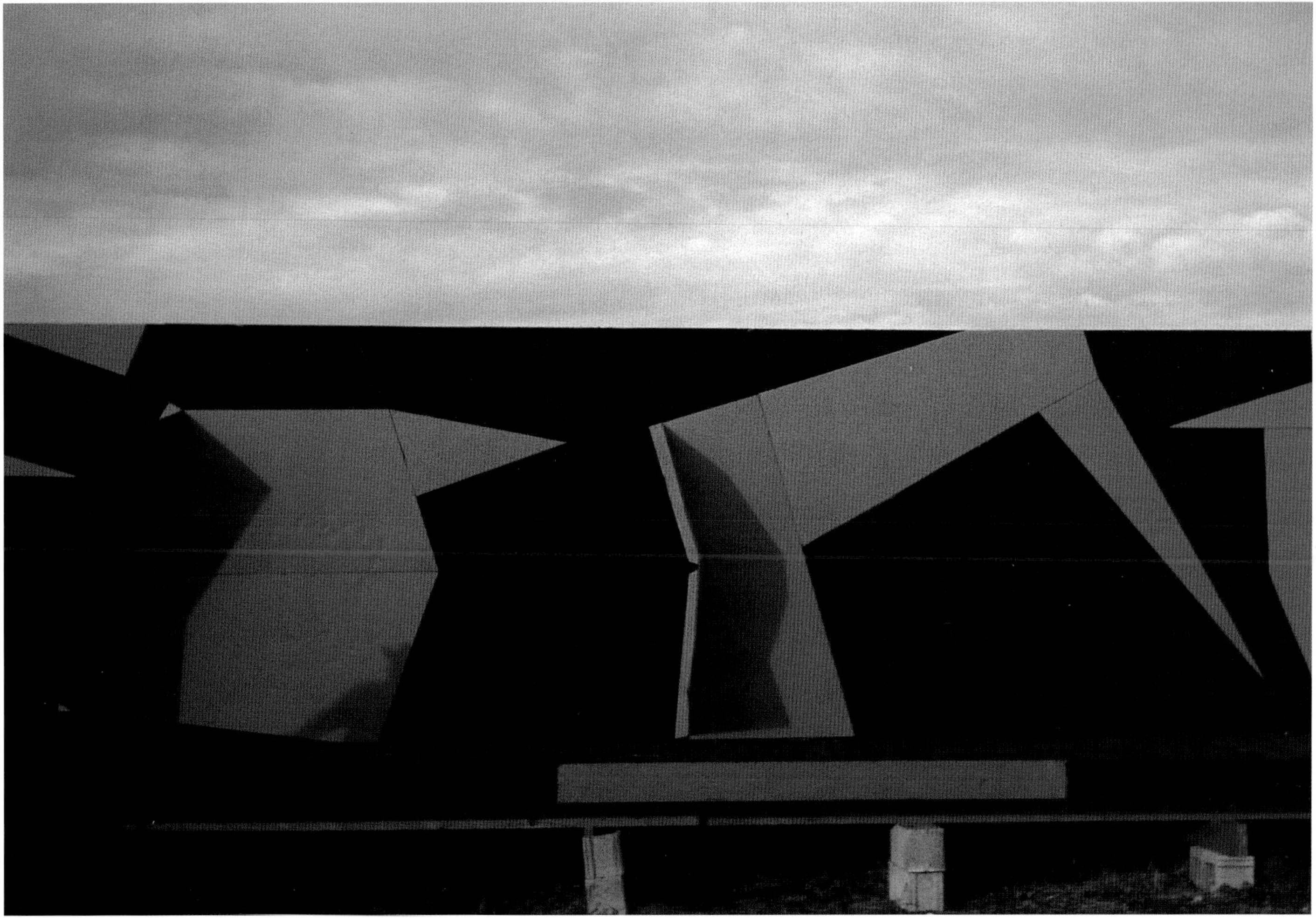

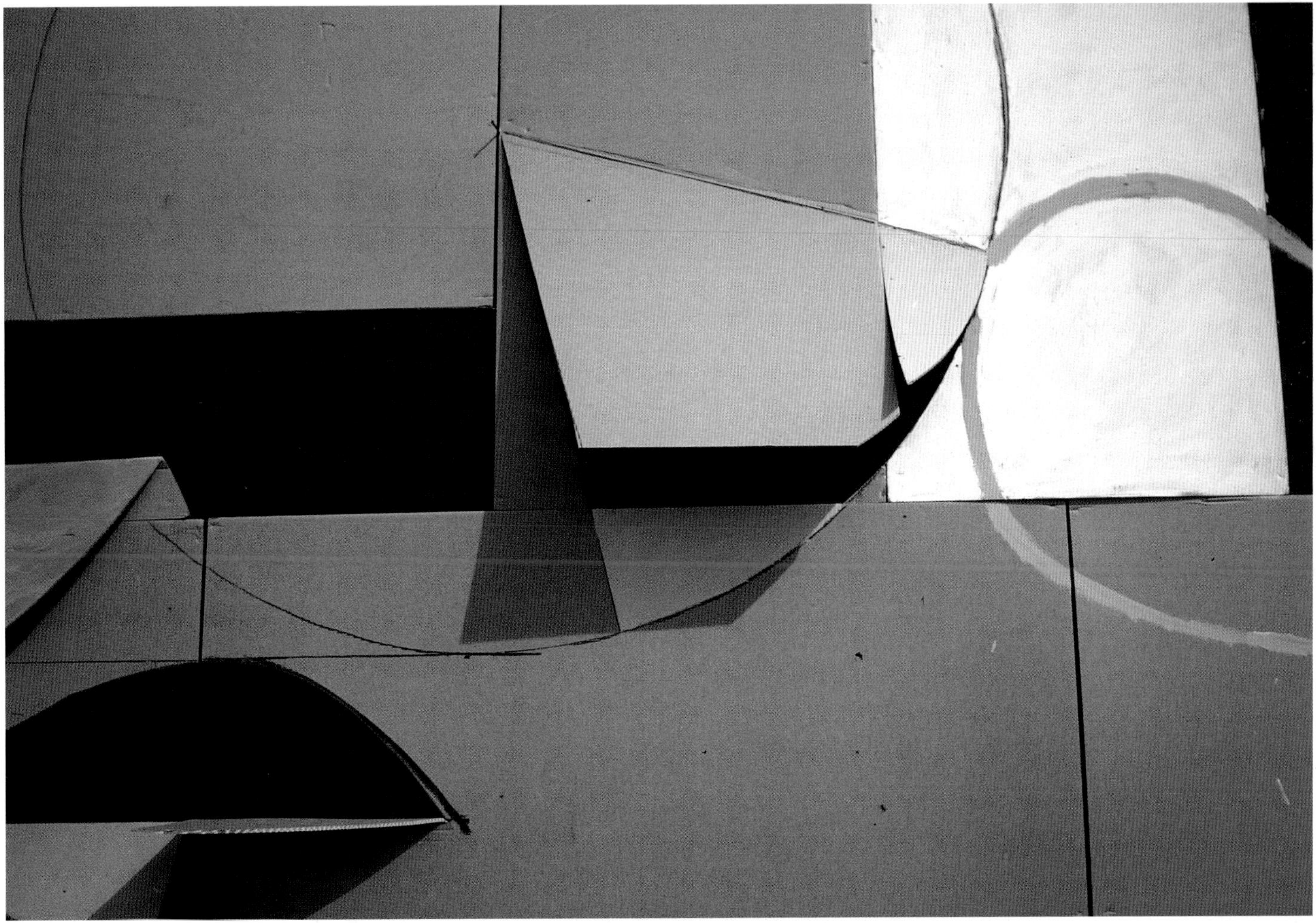

a   designer traffic jam
a   concept car park
        art park pay and display
        celebration of an intersection
        orchestrated bumper to bumper road rage
        and programmed lorry-load shedding diversion scheme on flyover
        underpass and dual carriageway gridlock situation
        asleeping policeman enforcement camera
                    black   spot
                    red   routed
                    red   light
        double   yellow   street painting
        with   white   reflector cats eyes and radar trap highway coded
        conical cone line collision
        afilter laned
        no entry
        congested polluted
        sin plomo'd
        sans plomed
        insensitive scenario for a weekend highway siren symphony
        chock
a   block
        installation